T0042927

BLACK HEART  FADES BLUE

Vol. 3

JERRY A. LANG

with George P. Lewis

RARE BIRD

Los Angeles, Calif.

THIS IS A GENUINE RARE BIRD BOOK

Rare Bird Books
453 South Spring Street, Suite 302
Los Angeles, CA 90013
rarebirdbooks.com

Copyright © 2022 by Jerry A. Lang

All rights reserved, including the right to reproduce this book or portions thereof
in any form whatsoever, including but not limited to print, audio, and electronic.
For more information, address:
Rare Bird Books Subsidiary Rights Department
453 South Spring Street, Suite 302
Los Angeles, CA 90013.

Set in Dante
Printed in the United States

10 9 8 7 6 5 4 3 2 1

Publisher's Cataloging-in-Publication data available upon request.

THANKS—To Adam Parfrey, for first hearing the rhythm of it. Tom Roberts, for convincing me it was worth it. Tyson, for seconding the motion. Jeff Larsen, for helping me take it out of the box, and George Pavlids, for helping me assemble it. Juxe Areta Goni, for the cover photograph. This is dedicated to Jennifer.

WHAT YOU HAVE IN YOUR hand is volume number three of a three-volume set. One and two came before this and you should read both before starting this one. In all honesty, if you don't have one and two, you'll at least know how the story ends, and it's a fun read. But that would be like eating your dessert first and skipping your dinner. Volume one has happy baby Jerry on the cover, volume two has bloody teenage Jerry. And this book, volume three, has adult Jerry on the cover. Do I look happy? Every day above ground makes me happy. Not to give the story away, "Bloody teenage Jerry." Feel free to use that for a band name. If you have to explain a joke, it's not funny.

1

THE DRUG SPIRAL HAD GONE on long enough. It was music that had been my first love, and I longed for the day it would again come first. Before I move this story along to my battle with addiction, I want to talk about my other bands.

Over the years, there have been a lot of good bands in Portland that are today long forgotten. I've played in more than a dozen bands myself, and I think a few of them were pretty good. There was Jungle Nausea, which was sort of like the Contortions but a little more tribal like Bow Wow Wow. I actually got kicked out of that band. I was tripping during a show at the Clinton Street Theater and people were throwing ice cubes at me. My eyes were spinning in my head at that show and the rest of the band decided they didn't want to put up with my problems anymore, they'd had enough. Another one of my short-lived bands was called The SIDS. The name was kind of a play on both the many Sid Vicious wannabes and sudden infant death syndrome. I could imagine a music critic describing us as being angular. All I know is that it was a fun group to play in. We'd improv songs and make up lyrics like "Car Crash / Black Sky / Busted Light" based on things we were seeing before our eyes.

In addition to those bands, I've done time in Smegma, The Kinetics, The Stand, Pisswild Horses, SWAT, Gumby Anti-Christ, and Gift. I've collaborated with Dare to Defy, Killer of Sheep,

Anti-Seen, 25th Coming Five, Jenny Don't & the Spurs, The Phantom Notes, The Ransoms, and Decimation Front. I practiced with some bands when I was down in SF that I never joined, including Bad Posture. I've been a one-time Elvis impersonator. I've performed with the Hard-Ons, Big Stick, Brad Boatwright, The Nightbirds, and The Eyelids. There have been a few projects that didn't quite work out. For instance, Jeff Dahl from The Angry Samoans came and made a record with the band. I think he might have stayed with Tom for a few days, though I'm not sure. I was supposed to go in the studio with Jeff and the band and cover some Dead Boys songs, but things kept getting in the way, namely my drug habit. So I did miss out on that experience, unfortunately, and it wasn't the only missed opportunity. Recently, there's been talk of collaborating on something with Paul Bearer from Sheer Terror. I think that could be interesting. Yes, Poison Idea is my main group, the one I poured my heart and soul into, but I've enjoyed other musical alliances and experiences.

Many bands are lost to history. That said, quite a few local bands broke out in the nineties and two thousands, and they kind of put Portland on the map. Some broke big, and probably contributed to putting the city on the hipster trail, along with places like Brooklyn, Austin, and San Francisco. Some of these bands I like and some not so much. But I know lots of stories. As I'm writing this book, I have a podcast that I do every Friday morning on House of Sound, a cool, free-form nonprofit radio station that advertises as being Portland's only uncensored radio. I've thought about telling some of those stories on internet radio but haven't yet.

Here's just one example. There's a big local rock star who is a compulsive liar. I'll protect his identity here. I know a guy who went on tour with his band as part of the road crew. They were playing a big arena and backstage one member of the road crew began talking about what it was like when he lived in South Central LA. How it was such a dangerous neighborhood. Then he related a wild story about a huge gas leak. It was so big that it blew out every window in the immediate vicinity, and it killed a guy by blowing his head clean off his body. The head was found four blocks away. The big rock star listened intently as the story was being told. Then he did his sound check and left for a meal break. A few hours later, he's back in the dressing room, talking to the road crew and part of his inner circle, and maybe a few fans who had gotten backstage. And he says, "Did I ever tell any of you about the time when I lived in South Central?" And then he proceeded to tell the roadie's story word for word as if it were his own. The crew kind of laughed along nervously at first. They thought he was just fucking around and would acknowledge the source. But he never did, and they began to realize he believed what he was saying. He was just plain crazy.

How was PI doing at this time? Well, when the crazy rock star was lying his ass off and playing coliseums, I got a royalty check from Italy. It turned out that some band I had never heard of had covered one of our songs. How much was it for? I think it was a dollar and fifty-one cents. It wasn't even worth cashing. Like I had told Wurzel from Motörhead, we weren't getting rich doing this. By chance, the day it arrived, I got a mail-order request from some kid who wrote that he was a big fan. When I filled his order, I enclosed the royalty check, thinking it might be a cool souvenir for someone who really liked the band. I'd sometimes do that, if I had something cool lying around that would be a unique memento. It might be a cut-and-paste collage I had made, or a postcard of Black Bart with one of his bandit poems, or an old show flyer of, say, a Scratch Acid/Hell Cows show that definitely had some history, whatever was handy. I tried to imagine what it might have been like for me to get a relic like that from, say, Johnny Cash or The Kinks.

2

JAPAN. I MADE A BRIEF ALLUSION to Japan earlier in this tale of woe. But I didn't say much about it, so why not here.

I got clued into Japanese hardcore pretty early on. Tom and I knew of some of the older punk and new wave bands like The Stalin and The Plastics (who had even toured the US and performed on American TV). But then we started hearing early hardcore, plus more experimental noise bands like Hidjokaidan, Hanatarashi, and Merzbow. Pretty extreme stuff. The music would come to us from many sources. I think Pushead turned us on to some of the bands. The underground was a small world unto itself. Tom and I each had the ultra-rare flexi single by State Children, a head-peeling record that would sound like utter noise to almost everyone, but which is worth a small fortune today. By that point, we had begun keeping our ears pointed to Japan. They didn't influence us and we didn't influence them, but we appreciated what they were doing. You could hear some influences, like early Discharge, in Japcore. But it really was its own unique thing. People from other scenes have told me that punks in Portland were more up on what was going on in Japan. Maybe geography had something to do with it: Portland is almost exactly the same distance from London and Tokyo. Actually, I think we're about seventy-five miles closer to Tokyo.

Sure, bands everywhere build on inspirations and influences. This is true from Des Moines, Iowa, to Dunedin, New Zealand. But we tried to make it our own and put our own stamp on it. There were other international punk scenes we followed. There were a lot of good bands in Italy, Norway, and Sweden, for example. Tom was also fond of the German and Dutch scenes. I was more into the Finnish stuff, and was especially big on the band Lama. But as a scene, Japan stood out. The most extreme stuff sounded pretty ferocious; by comparison, I always thought our music was more melodic and structured.

Of the first wave of punk bands, The Stalin was my favorite. The singer was a guy named Michiro Endo who seemed pretty unique. He was a lot older, and he had lived a full life before punk rock. He would later become a kind of a folky punk troubadour, maybe Bob Dylan–like in some ways. He had something to do with a fanzine called *Ingo*. Yes, occasionally Japanese music magazines would make their way to Portland, and we liked looking through them, even if we couldn't read the language. *Doll* was a popular one. A picture is worth a thousand words. Our favorite Japanese hardcore band was Gism—whose name was an acronym with many different meanings. I didn't really get it at first. They were too metal for my taste, but I would come around. They were so extreme. They were talented musicians and, by all accounts, their live shows were dangerous. They made a strong impression. Their singer, Sakevi, made noise collages and put out magazines like *POW* that were like works of art. He was also known for being a legendary fighter. Occasionally there would be a musician with a reputation. People in LA used to talk about John Macias that way. A guy not to be messed with. Sakevi had that reputation in Tokyo.

Because of our long-standing interest, Tom and I had wanted to play shows in Japan. Tom was a big-time tape trader and people would send him mixtapes of Japcore that also included Japanese metal and sixties GS (Group Sounds) bands. So we were up on some of that stuff. That was kind of how it was with Australia, too. It was a primitive social network. Though our fascination with Japanese music was at its zenith in the eighties and early nineties, I kept up a little bit. A friend of mine in NYC would go to Japan often, and he'd send me fanzines, albums, flyers, and movies. He'd usually bring back copies of *Burst* magazine, which was kind of similar to the British subculture magazine *Bizarre*. Through him, I'd find out the latest news. For instance, we were talking about the band Inu one time and I learned that the singer had become a novelist who had won major literary awards.

You know, I probably wanted to go to Japan when I first saw Japanese imports of Kiss records when I was a kid. That's probably where it started. Some records had cool looking "obi" strips along the side and some albums by American and British bands might have had an extra track or two for the Japanese audience, which made them a prized possession for fans in the States. Cheap Trick made a famous live album recorded at Budokan. And I remember seeing photos of The Runaways, who were treated like big stars in Japan when they were barely known in America. There was also a connection between Japan and the No Wave scene in New York. Japanese musicians had been in DNA and Teenage Jesus & the Jerks. One of them had returned to Japan and started a cool band called Friction.

So although we were all strung out on dope, we booked a tour of Japan. I had seen enough Japanese gangster movies that I figured I could go into some sleazy punk bar and buy enough dope to take care of me for the entire tour. In preparation, I did a large amount before I flew out of Portland. Not enough to OD, but more than enough to keep me well for the half-day flight. Dope has legs, so I didn't get sick right away. I think we played a show the same day we landed, so I just slammed a bottle of Japanese whiskey and did the gig. No problem. But once the drugs were completely out of my system, I had to start putting in some work, pestering everyone who would talk to me (in broken English), asking about heroin. Between the pills that the local kids gave me that had enough opiates in them and copious amounts of booze, I lasted about two to three days before turning desperate.

One of our minders was—well, I'm not gonna assume anything, especially in this department, but he was tattooed from the neck all the way down, and his people showed him tremendous respect wherever we went. I do know tattoos are often equated with yakuza, though I've also heard stories of innocent garage rock people not being allowed to go swimming in a public pool because they have tattoos. There was talk that our handler was a member of a Japanese organized crime gang, but since he never directly told me that himself, I'm not going to assume anything. I got along with him fine, and why shouldn't I?

In one major city, I asked around and people told me where to buy drugs. It was down the street from where we were gonna play that night. I could even see it from the top floor of the building where the concert was held. But they said it was too dangerous an area, nobody goes down this street at night. I could see the alley that people had pointed out to me. All I knew was it was the place to buy drugs but it was considered too dangerous to walk down that street. So I asked our tattooed helper if he knew where I could buy heroin. He said he knew where to get some, but in that town you had to deal with Persians for heroin, and if he were to do that, he'd owe them a big favor. I said no, I would owe *him* a favor, a big favor for doing this, thank you for doing this. I'm really grateful. No, he said, he couldn't do it, because then he would owe the Persians a favor. I wondered if I could owe them (the Persians) a favor. Could I? No. We went back and forth for a couple of minutes, and I never could figure out what was going on. It might have sounded like Abbott and Costello's *Who's on First* routine.

Now I can guess the gist of it was if he was gonna ask a favor, it better be worth it and this wasn't. He'd be the one who owed them, and they'd come back to collect on it some day. There were supposedly drugs right down the street, but I had been warned against that. Maybe you couldn't buy them without getting grabbed and sold into slavery or something? Well, that would certainly be an incentive not to ever do dope again. Then again, at the time I was considering that option, I was already a slave to it.

What about all those Takashi Miike movies I'd watched, where gangsters run all over slamming dope into every part of their body? Not only gangsters, but schoolgirls and rockers. Dope was so common in these movies. Ah, they're fucking movies, I get it now. I was more likely to see Godzilla jump out of the bay than find heroin in Japan.

By this point, the promoters and handlers realized that they flew a band over to Japan to perform and make money for them, but the singer was strung-out and needed his daily drug allotment. They had all sorts of psychotropic drugs over there, more than any mental patient could swallow, but they wouldn't do shit for me in my condition. These firings in my brain were from another section. The closest thing they could come up with was this stuff called BRON. It was kind of a cross between Robotussin and codeine cough syrup. At one time it was full of codeine, but that created an army of degenerates called "Bron bums" who would swig the stuff and stay loaded. As my luck would have it, they cut out almost all of the codeine. There was some, maybe 12 percent or so? Enough that if I bought cases of it, spent every yen I had, and went to every pharmacy and bought them out, well, then I could almost stay well. I had to drink enough to keep from going into full-blown withdrawal and then start chugging as much Japanese whiskey as I could hold down so that I could halfway function. As a result, even someone like Shane McGowan would have been embarrassed and ashamed by my performances.

It wasn't all bad. We met some nice people in every city and played with some great musicians. I can't remember all the bands, but there were guys who had been in Gism and Deathside, both of whom had been big in the international hardcore scene, plus bands like Melt-Banana who have an international following. There were many bands I had not heard before (or since) that I enjoyed. We were on some good bills.

People ask if we met Gauze, Cobra, Systematic Death, Kuro, S.O.B., The Comes, Lip Cream, Outo, Corrupted, Idora, Aburadako, Casbah, Bastard, etc. Or if we met this garage band or that noise band. Well, we met a lot of people, but I'm not sure of all the connections. In my state, it was kind of hard to keep track. We didn't get to meet a lot of the early bands, many had broken up. Of course, I got to meet Sakevi. I suppose it was like the meeting of two mob bosses when I went backstage and paid him respect. I joked to a friend that it would be like a scene in *The Sopranos* where Tony kisses the ring of the boss of bosses, with all our people surrounding us. Poison Idea had covered some Gism songs and I wanted him to know how much those records meant to us. Sadly, the guitarist Randy Uchida had passed away from cancer. It would have been great to meet him.

One of the oddest moments on tour was when our translator came up to me bleeding profusely. I asked what had happened, but he wouldn't tell me. It would be quite some time before he would open up. To be precise, it took more than a few drinks later in the tour to drag it out of him.

It turns out that he had gone backstage after the show. He wound up getting into a conversation with Sakevi. When Sakevi asked him what he thought of his set that night, the translator said something along the lines of "I've seen better. The old stuff was great. This stuff isn't. You've lost your edge." He then continued to run Sakevi down. "You used to be so violent and dangerous, look at you now." As he's telling me this, I'm thinking OMG! Doesn't he know the reputation? He has to know. After taking enough of the translator's insults, Sakevi finally had enough. He must have gone all Mike Tyson on the guy. Pow Pow! A three- or four-shot combination splitting the translator's face open. Or maybe it was a headbutt? It was unfortunate it happened, but Sakevi's reaction is understandable after an unprovoked attack of offensive insults. I remember thinking maybe I'd have reacted the same way if I was riding the bus and some stranger came up and started insulting me. The translator should have known better: it was like he was asking for it. You don't poke a bear.

Personally, I actually dug a lot of Sakevi's solo stuff as much as the Gism stuff. It was so cool and extreme. We enjoyed covering Gism songs like "Endless Blockades for the Pussyfooter" and "Death Agonies and Screams," but I liked his solo every bit as much, if not more. The kicker to the story is that the bloodied translator had to go back after getting his ass kicked and bow down and apologize. His insult had violated the Japanese code of conduct, and he had to make public amends.

We played with musicians who had been in legendary Japcore bands from the eighties. Again, I don't remember the exact lineage, though I was told about it at the time. I know the sound guy one night had been in a cool band. The owner or manager of a watering hole we visited had been in a band whose songs I knew. It was cool like that. And it happens all over. In Europe and Australia, too. Your bartender or the doorman may have written a song that meant a lot to you. Sometimes meeting musicians whose music you like can be disappointing. Maybe even most of the time. But in Japan, those experiences were almost all good.

After one show, we were told a wealthy fan wanted to take care of our drinks for the night. A thousand dollars later, we found out that this fan was kind and generous but not wealthy. Our drinking had cleaned him out. Maybe something had been lost in the translation. Hell, blame it on the translation, our translator was probably already drunk! Maybe we thought he was the bar owner? Or maybe he never imagined we could drink so much. Still, he made the offer and was stuck with an astronomical bar tab. Whatever the case, I've always wanted to apologize for the misunderstanding and thank him again for his generosity.

I could never figure out the Japanese way. The rest of the band was stomping around, refusing to take off their shoes when entering houses. It was going right over their heads. Maybe because I was borderline sober, I think I noticed people hissing at us. I was never straight-out rude, but some people gave me the stink eye about the band not following Japanese customs (taking off shoes, etc.). We played with more than a handful of bands who have toured the US, and I later saw some snapshots of one of them flashing their asses and flipping off statues, whatever. I don't care, but it seems like a double standard.

At one club, the combo of Bron and a liter of whiskey wasn't working too well. I then made the mistake of having a couple rounds of sake after we played. I was sitting at a table feeling like death, and I could feel that sensation in my mouth that could only mean vomit was right behind it. Before I could stand up, everything that was inside me came up. And it hadn't even started to digest. It was straight whiskey; I could have puked it right back into the bottle and no one would have known it came from my stomach. Glasses, pints, quarts, gallons, splashed out. An overflowing river of stinking strong straight booze. The Japanese person I was with grabbed me by the arm and quickly hustled me out the door. When I got outside, I saw the second handler. He asked what happened. I told him, and he exploded: "You didn't clean it up?!" One guy grabs me and runs me out before anyone says anything, the next guy is waiting outside to bitch at me for leaving so quickly. I never figured out what the fuck was going on. I know they greatly value respect and honor.

We played a show in the city of Hiroshima. A couple of the promoters took me aside and asked if I would make a speech before our set and apologize for dropping the atomic bomb almost seventy years earlier. I argued that I had nothing to do with that, and while I certainly didn't agree that it should have happened, it was a war, and war is hell, etc. They pushed the issue. Like the Germans, who insist on you going back and doing encore after encore just to let you know who is in charge, I felt I had to do this. Hell, maybe they would owe me a favor. Maybe they know some Persians. Ah, no such luck.

I get up onstage, suck it up, and tell the audience what they all wanted to hear—that I was sorry that someone I didn't know dropped a bomb on other people that I didn't know.

There were times when fans would come up to me crying, saying they never thought we'd come to Japan and that they'd never be able to meet me in person. It was humbling and touching, even though I was usually blitzed out of my mind. One young woman saw us a few times. We talked a bit each night and after the final show she handed me a long handwritten letter. I promised her I would have it translated and would write back. When I got back to the States, I had a Japanese friend in NYC translate it. Basically, this girl wanted me to know that we were her favorite band and that our songs had helped her get through rough times. I've heard this more than a few times over the years. (For instance, I remember a guy coming up to me in front of CBGB's telling me our songs helped him get through prison and that another friend who was still in the joint was a big PI fan and wanted to say hello.) This stuff is always touching, but this was a little different. Though this girl was very hardcore, and dressed the part, the letter was written on cutesy Japanese stationary. It was a combination that I found charmingly innocent and genuine. It was a sweet letter. Sadly, I lost the address and never did write. But maybe acknowledging it here is better than nothing?

One thing I'd like to do before PI calls it quits is to go back to Japan and play shows sober and at full strength. I'm really kind of embarrassed and disappointed by some of our performances. It still feels like unfinished business. I'd also like to go back so I can see more of the country and maybe learn more about Japanese etiquette and way of life.

The night before we left we went out to get tattoos in a famous tattoo parlor in Tokyo. The shop was known for its high quality and specialized in elaborate dragons, samurai, and Japanese kanji. With all this to choose from, what did I get? I got the word BRON tattooed in Japanese on my right wrist. The Japanese Robotussin. After we were inked up, they paid us what tour money we had made from merchandise, playing live, and selling rights to our live recordings for future releases.

We got on a plane, bought quarts of duty-free alcohol, and drank until we were met in Portland by airport security and Federal Marshalls. You see, one of us, not me (believe it or not), was handcuffed to a wheelchair and escorted off the plane. I ducked

like a down-to-earth guy, his main gig was food. I had a couple of years working in the food industry, and I cooked for my brother and sister when I helped raise them. Whenever I hear people talk about not knowing how to cook, it always blows me away. Prepping a five-course meal is one thing, but boiling water, toasting bread, and mixing a few ingredients in a bowl is something everyone should know how to do. This was once something they taught in schools; now they teach students where the escape exits are.

Besides wanting to pick Anthony Bourdain's brain about chicken knuckles, I have so many questions he could have answered. Just by describing a dish to him, he could have identified it and cleared up a mystery. Touring with bands over the years, I did my share of having the road crew run out and pick up whatever they could find on the street to keep me going until the next city. But I also put in a decent amount of research and exploring on my own. And then trying things I wasn't sure of. Mystery dishes. In Australia, I was tripping out of my mind on LSD one night, stumbling around. I found this kebab stand with what looked like souvlaki meat on a turning spit. You would order what you want, with or without salad (which in this case pretty much meant lettuce), and then they would add strange sauce, purple cabbage, and onions, and wrap it up. It was a pocket food, like a burrito or other food you can eat walking around. It was a fast operation. You could be out of there in under a minute. The meat had hardly any fat on it, and I couldn't place the taste. It wasn't spiced beef, chicken, lamb, or ground-up pork. I wondered if it was a combination, with some filler added? I was so high, I ate about half of it and smeared the other half down the front of my shirt. When the Hard-Ons picked me up the next morning at my hotel, they told me it was kangaroo meat. I didn't believe them. They insisted this was a well-known fact when it came to sketchy Sydney street food. I still don't know if it really was kangaroo or if they were just fucking with me. Anthony Bourdain would have known.

In Germany and Austria, the food carts in the street were already big when I first went there. Street vendors, with their food carts, are now pretty common in many big American cities. Portland actually now has a thriving scene downtown, and it caught on here before it did in many American cities. It was rare then, but some European countries had it going on. Fresh baked rolls, homemade bratwursts grilled right in front of you. And there was a dildo-looking pole where they would rip the tip off the bun, shove it on the elevated three-foot-long metal dildo, hollowing out the bun in the process, and then they'd squirt a shot of spicy mustard inside and shove the brat behind it. And you were out of there in thirty seconds. Germany: the head cheese, the blood-sausage. The raw cured bacon, raw pork. I'm sure Anthony Bourdain could explain why this works, and I didn't die from eating it.

As for the Basque Country, I could impress him with my culinary knowledge just by telling him what we ate at one restaurant. The seafood, the paella, the tapas, the ice cream cake with the baked bourbon whiskey glaze, the squid cooked in its own smoky black ink!

Like everything in Japan, I loved it but I didn't understand it completely. There were convenience stores that looked pretty much like a 7-Eleven where they had a giant boiling cauldron in the center of the room full of bubbling broth and dumplings along with some assorted meats and something that looked like cabbage. You would tell them what you wanted and they would ladle out this liquid and throw in whatever else you wanted to include. And as they would take broth out, they would add what looked like scraps to replenish the mix. The rest of the store was four walls, with maybe four large wall-to-wall coolers full of sushi. No gum, cigarettes, or beer. It looked like a 7-Eleven, but this was more like a broth store. Not even a Big Gulp. And then there was the big twelve-course meal I was taken to by the Japanese tour promoter, in the height of my heroin withdrawal. OMG! That food. I could talk with Anthony Bourdain about that alone for an hour. I later learned it was a kaiseki meal. Who knows how many ingredients were used in that? Most of it was very refined. Though I might ask about the raw egg that was presented as one of the courses. There was so much food. I kept going to the bathroom and vomiting but I didn't want my hosts to know. That would have been really bad.

The curries in London! And the States? The cheesesteaks, lobster rolls, Andouille sausage, fried chicken and waffles, BBQ, soft-shelled blue crab, the food along the southern border! Jeez, I got a lot of questions about food, a lot of opinions, and a lot of stories about the creations I've concocted in the kitchen. This stuff? I guess I'll have to add it to all that digested food that I've flushed down the shitter. RIP Anthony Bourdain.

Travel can be a great education. In terms of seeing art, architecture, the way people live, the culture, different societies. Hearing local idioms and regional dialects. Sampling the culinary offerings. But then it would always be back to Portland and the old ways, the old demons.

be the Blind Faith album. I must have been ten or eleven when I got that. Another band from England that was huge for me was Sparks. Actually, the band is from LA but they were living in England when I first discovered them, and many people assumed they were English. The first time I heard them was a definite "what the fuck?" moment. But I liked them from the start. The Mael brothers have written so many great songs, and they still are to this day.

Manchester was special to me because of what it has given the world—the music, the culture. There was a little bit more of a bounce in my step when we passed through town. One time we played there in a big venue in a grimy, industrial part of the city. It was a large three-story place, and you had to walk up a hill to get to it. It was kind of a state-of-the-art club. This place was outfitted with high-tech security cameras. The bartenders had the use of a machine that measured out drinks, probably slightly to the advantage of the club. Maybe not quite a full pour, and the drinks were overpriced to start with, maybe nine pounds for a drink. The house always wins.

I don't remember much about the show at this particular club, other than it being decent. But there was something that made it memorable. Beforehand, I had gone out looking for speed. The guy who went with me took me to an apartment building where we met a member of The Happy Mondays and got what we had come for. So I returned to the club and started wandering around, exploring every nook and cranny. I found myself in some recess of the place, in a hallway near an emergency door. I heard a sound coming from the other side of this big door. I was curious, so I went to investigate. As I walked over, the voices were getting louder and louder. There was an opening in the middle of the door that was thin like a mail slot. When I leaned down and looked through it, I saw a bunch of teenagers, and then I realized they had been loudly pleading for me to let them in. "We're too young. They won't let us in."

I've always been empathetic to kids who come to our shows and can't make it in due to lack of funds, the event being sold-out, or club policy. We all remember not being able to get into shows when we were young. Tom always remembered that time he couldn't see The Ramones even when he had a ticket because when he bought the advance ticket no one had told him he had to be twenty-one to actually use it. He had been so upset after he was turned away at the door that he went to a pay phone, deepened his voice, and called in a bomb threat. "You better shut that mother down, because that place is gonna blow up!" Of course, that club didn't do shit. A little old bomb wasn't gonna stand in the way of good profit. But it was probably cathartic for Tom—a funny way to release hostility. So, yeah, as a band, we were pretty sympathetic to kids who couldn't get into shows because of age restrictions.

But when I looked at this heavy door that was bolted shut, with a sign prominently displayed that said "Alarm Will Sound," I wasn't sure what to do. I had to talk with the kids through the slot. I told them to hold on while I went to scope out the place. I quickly looked around, the coast was clear, so I came back. "All right, I'll open the door, the alarm is gonna go off, so when I hit it, you motherfuckers be ready to run as fast as you can!" I even counted it down: three-two-one. Blam! I busted open the door and the alarm rang out. "Go, go, go!" The kids blasted in. Well, all except one. This one kid just stood there, staring blankly. He didn't do shit. I held the door for a few extra seconds, waiting for him to get a move on. We made eye contact. "Come on, let's go, let's go! Come on!" But he just stood there. The alarm was still blaring, and it was deafening. "Last chance." He did nothing, so I let go of the door. As fast as I could, I ran up the three flights of stairs to our dressing room. The band was all there, and as I rushed in huffing and puffing, they wanted to know what was up. I sat down, too exhausted to utter a word.

5

"Breaking beds across Europe"—that was one of our mottos. There are many road stories from Europe. If I ever were to do a spoken word thing there would be lots to choose from, from having wild performance artists open a show to people having sex onstage to riotous conditions and buildings shaking in bedlam. It would take a big book to tell them all, but I'll give a small sampling here.

It's still a trip to play big shows or festivals in Europe. I have to pinch myself sometimes. When I was a kid growing up in small towns in Oregon and Montana, it was hard to imagine seeing another part of the world. Maybe I could have imagined traveling to Boise, Idaho, but not Bristol, England. Little did I know when I was watching *James Bond* movies as a kid that I would actually be able to see Monte Carlo in person.

We were playing a show in Germany once when I was hit by a full-pint glass. I continued singing but kept one eye open for another projectile. Sure enough, I see another one come sailing from the balcony. It whizzes by me. I drop the mic, say, "That's it!" and run up the stairs. Justice would be swift. I grab the guy that I think threw it and then the soundman screams, "No, no, not him!" He then points at another guy, a giant biker. "That guy threw it." Fuck. So, despite his size, I go charging after the guy. I punch him in the face. Before I know it, four of his friends jump on me and the five of them start wailing. My kid brother, who was working with us, quickly ran to my defense. Luckily for me, he's fast as lightning. If not, I would have taken a lot more blows. At some point, we go back-to-back and start taking on these guys. My brother is smaller than me but he had a few things going for him: he was very fit from a life of hard work...he knew how to fight (and how to take a punch, which is an overlooked skill)...and he was full of piss and vinegar. He also had twice the energy I did. And we both had a surplus of adrenaline. We took on these five bikers and laid them out. As we made our way back toward the stage, my brother pointed to his crotch, and I saw a chalk boot outline where someone had stomped on him with their Doc Martens. He had been so pumped up that I doubt he felt anything.

There have been logistical challenges on some of these tours. Twice in Europe we suffered through a "once in a century heatwave." How's that for bad luck? When our van didn't have AC it was like we were baking in an oven. We also once had a booking agency who created an obstacle tour from hell. We'd go 400 miles in one direction and then come back 500 miles, then go 400 miles in a totally different direction. The scale is different but imagine playing one night in Seattle, the next night in Miami, followed by San Diego, Boston, and Houston—that would be insane. We probably spent twice as much time in the van as we needed to. We should have been paid by the mile. Every city seemed out of the way. We'd be crossing back through a country multiple times without actually playing a show. It was as if they took a map and randomly picked cities and then drew a pentagram connecting them. It was a nightmare.

Of course, complicating matters on these long European death marches was our own addiction issues. Tom needed methadone when we were in Germany. And a doctor was sent to a hospital where he examined Tom and prescribed twenty meth tablets. Those didn't last long since it got divided up by members of the band.

Doctors and pharmacists in Europe would often question my US prescriptions. "There is no reason for you to be taking this. It does nothing. It actually may be doing you more harm than good. You are wasting your money. You should be taking a different medication." When I'd report these comments back home, the medical people would say the Europeans didn't know what they were talking about. But after I had experienced this a number of times, it dawned on me that the Europeans were probably right and the reason for some of the prescriptions could be traced back to the role of the big pharmaceutical companies in our healthcare system. Big Pharma doesn't want you to look behind the curtain.

I've always enjoyed traveling and seeing the world. You'll often hear that touring bands only drive to the venue, play a show, drive to the hotel, and then repeat that cycle the next day. While there's a lot of truth in that, I do try to make an effort to go out and see things. I like to check out record shops, get a sense of the geography, visit historical sites, sample the local food, mingle with clubgoers, and make new friends. I like to see how people live. The day-to-day existence, how it's different from my own experience. What can I learn and use in my own life? I was hungry for culture when I was growing up poor in an isolated place like Deer Lodge, and I still am. I like seeing the culture and meeting locals. Of course, when I was chasing drugs all over Europe, I wasn't seeing much outside that world.

Music is a universal language. There have been beautiful moments in places like Belgium and Hungary where I could not speak the language but could bond with strangers over music we loved. Maybe you're walking down the street and see a bunch of young kids listening to a collection of punk anthems, pumping fists and banging heads, and it takes you back to your adolescence. Maybe they are experiencing the Ramones the way you did when you were fourteen, when it was all fresh and new. Maybe you even stop and sing a line or two.

I could describe all of the beautiful art I have seen. The old cathedrals, the world-class museums, amazing murals, and graffiti. Or I could talk about the torture museums in Amsterdam and Prague. Man has experimented for centuries with how to make others suffer. We have excelled in that; we know when to turn the gas up. The Dark Ages do not always seem far away.

I'll mention the drug market in Oslo. Getting up at 7:00 a.m. and standing in line with a hundred other dope fiends. The police turned a blind eye. It felt more like a soup kitchen with dealers ladling out the daily dose. When it was my turn, I asked if I bought a large amount, would I get a discount? The dealers said, "Sure!" So we bought at least $500 worth and burned through it all really fast. Our habits got twice as big. We put the pedal to the medal, but we were heading in the wrong direction.

Given the challenges of touring, it can be a pleasant surprise to make friends or run into old friends on the road. One time we flew into Munich and were setting out on our European tour the next day. We were looking for something to do that night just to pass the time. One of our contacts told us "a band you've probably never heard of is playing across the street tonight." I was stoked when it turned out to be Leatherface, a band whose records I knew and liked. We went to the show, hung out with the band afterward, had a great time, and became instant friends. Our paths would cross more times over the years and it was always great to see them.

We'd take a bunch of stuff to listen to or videos to watch on tours. We'd get mixtapes and CD samplers from people we'd meet, or bands we'd play with, and it wasn't unusual to encounter music I hadn't heard before. I can distinctly remember hearing the Pixies for the first time on a compilation CD we were given in the Midwest. They were doing something different but I wasn't crazy about it on first listen. Still, it made an impression. On an earlier Midwest tour we were given *Throb Throb* by Naked Raygun, which had just been released. I took to it immediately and played it over and over. I loved it. We almost wore it out. European tours could feel endless, and it was good to stock up for the long haul. We'd take all kinds of stuff. It could be a prank call cassette, like Lucious Tate. When it came to movies, it could be something like *Taxi Driver, Blue Velvet, The Godfather, Visitor Q, Begotten,* or *A Clockwork Orange.* Some of us learned practically every line of dialogue from *The Big Lebowski.* It was on constant repeat during one tour. We were a captive audience and it was enjoyed to the fullest. Another favorite was David Bowie's *Ziggy Stardust* concert film. The part of that rockumentary that never fails to blow my mind is when Bowie tells the audience that they are watching the last performance of The Spiders From Mars. Not only was it sad news to the audience that the band was breaking up, but it was *breaking news* to his bandmates! They were just blindsided, which had to be a total mindfuck.

We played many unusual and memorable venues in Europe. Once we played a big squat in France. I think it might have been shaped like a big barn, there was a place like that. What I most remember, though, was the smell of food. See, the band was starving and this food was obviously many steps beyond the cheap road grub we'd been living on. It was definitely a step up from packaged microwavable burritos. It turns out the hosts were frying up strip steaks! It had surprised me since they were tofu-eating hippies. Wow, this is great—Europeans *are* better hosts like people say. That's what I was thinking until I learned this aromatic feast was not intended for us. The hippies told us it was for their dogs! I had to wonder if these people were just twisting our caps. Well, it turned out the good eats *were* for Fido and Rover. I can't remember the particular gruel we were given for dinner, but I can guarantee you that those dogs did eat a lot better than we did.

In general, bands get treated better in Europe. Food and accommodations are often top-notch, sometimes a league above what most small bands are used to stateside. In the early days, cheap beer and a bag of chips would have satisfied us. Touring bands often have a contract rider. Basically, it's a list of things you request that a venue promises to make an attempt to provide. Maybe they can't fulfill the entire list but they should be able to make reasonable substitutes. Van Halen famously wanted no brown M&Ms, but the request was really just a way to make sure the venue had actually read the contract closely. James Brown supposedly wanted a hair dryer. Beer, champagne, deli trays are typical. Some people might ask for condoms. I heard Lee "Scratch" Perry wanted incense. One time we were a day or two behind a well-known garage band, playing many of the same venues. They requested new white socks and T-shirts. It was smart, practical. You don't have to do laundry as often or worry about how you smell traveling in cramped conditions. They'd always leave plenty behind, so we stocked up. Our own rider mostly involved alcohol. We'd list types of alcohol and sometimes specific brands. Gilby's gin, Bailey's Irish cream, Glenfiddich whiskey, a good brand of vanilla vodka. We'd ask for lots of ice and plenty of limes. Tom would sometimes put in a food request. It could be donuts, quiche, whatever he was craving at the time. We might get a buyout, meaning we'd be given money for food and could pick up whatever looked good close by. One time I was interviewed and was asked what I wanted while on the road or who would be the ideal sponsor of the band. My response was swift: "Black Death vodka!" I said it mostly because of the name itself; I thought it was funny. I don't think I'd even tried it at the time. A few days later, we showed up at a gig and found two complimentary cases of Black Death waiting for us. It was a goof that paid off. I guess I earned it, so I drank it up all by myself within a week.

On one of our later tours, we were in France, stuck in traffic in a sketchy area. Some guys approached our van to shake us down. There were more than a dozen watching from the wings, and some of them had makeshift weapons. These guys seemed like a cross between homeless guys and a gang. We heard about Corsican, North African, and Eastern European gangs; Middle Eastern refugees; and local homeless camps, but I couldn't tell you where these guys were from. One guy banged on the door, demanding money. Our driver waved him off. The guy then grabbed the large driver-side mirror between his arms. It was like he was carrying a football. He said he'd break it if we didn't give him twenty Euros. The driver didn't want to give in. For a minute or two, it became a Mexican standoff. But we could do the math. It would cost more than that to replace the mirror, plus we'd be stuck somewhere waiting for mechanics. It just was not worth it. Reluctantly, he rolled down the window and gave him the money. It was minor league extortion, but it sure felt like the country had changed since our previous visit—though maybe it was just our bad luck and the odds catching up to us.

There was a time we were in Germany, playing a big festival with popular new bands along with punk stalwarts, when some of the guys took to smashing the picture frames in the hallway of our hotel. They still believed in that tired old rock star cliché of throwing televisions out the windows into swimming pools. I suppose it was kind of cool when Keith Moon did it in 1968. That was then, this is now. This was a nice hotel. It also had security cameras which caught them in the act. We had to pay for the damage, which cut into most of what we had earned from the show. That was supposed to be a big payday but we basically played that concert for free.

Playing a lot of shows overseas can give a band the chance to hone their skills and develop their craft in different settings. But to take full advantage of the opportunity, everyone's got to be committed. A long tour can become a pressure cooker. If a guy starts to miss his girlfriend or over-indulge his substance issues, that'll be a problem. A wrench in your plans, another hurdle to clear. Though when everyone is on the same page and things are really clicking, it can be a tremendous rush, what you live for.

That time Tom quit the band in Europe, he wound up in London riding the tube and had a curious encounter. Maybe it was on the way to the airport. Tom was in bad shape at the time, and I'm not referring to his girth. He was dope sick, and he must have looked pretty bad. On the train, he was approached by a Hare Krishna woman. She didn't mention her name but said she had a punk past and recognized that he was part of the tribe. She implied that punk had at one time destroyed her life and suggested that he move on to something more life-affirming. Tom said she seemed genuinely concerned about his welfare. It was probably obvious that he was strung out, and he may have come across as self-destructive. Tom thought this woman was Poly Styrene, the singer from X-Ray Spex, a great London band from the late seventies. She had become a Hare Krishna and dropped out of the underground music world, so that would fit. She also had a pretty distinctive look and may have been relatively recognizable. Tom didn't ask her name. But he was convinced it was her, this woman looked just like her. I always wondered if he had been hallucinating but whenever I'd ask him, he'd swear he thought it was her. I'll never know.

Fallout from American foreign policy is something we've had to deal with. The band passed through Berlin at the beginning of the Gulf War. We checked into a giant hostel. Many of the guests were truck drivers from Islamic countries. If I had to guess, I'd wager most were from Turkey since Germany is home to many Turks, but probably some were Arabs from Persian Gulf countries. All I know is that they did not like the look of us. Hearing English being spoken, they asked if we were American. I didn't want to piss 'em off and create needless strife, so I said, "No, we're Canadians." They were puzzled at first, but they accepted that we were not villainous Americans and it eased the tension.

Traveling outside the US as often as we have, there have been numerous times I have met people who would be surprised to learn that I was an American. This happened in England once when I made a pilgrimage to where the Sex Pistols had their rehearsal space and had posed for a famous photo. A guy came out of the building and came out to talk with me. He said, "You have a different accent, you don't sound American." It turns out what he meant was that I was polite, and said "please" and "thank you." I guess many Americans he meets aren't respectful or don't display any manners. He invited me in and gave me a quick tour. So I suppose there is a reason for the "ugly American" stereotype. No matter how difficult the tour may be, or my own personal state due to substance abuse, I always made an effort to *not* be that stereotype. And I can't underscore that enough.

6

THERE WAS NO MOMENT OF clarity. I wasn't in some bathroom at McDonald's, shooting up, and saw myself in the mirror...*gasp*, or some stupid drama like that. I always had bad eyesight anyway. I didn't have a revelation by waking up in that basement and already feeling sick, first thing in the morning, looking toward the sky and asking out loud, "Why?" No epiphanies, no awakenings, this is something I thought about for quite a while. This had become boring. That's really about all there is to it. BUT (there's my big fucking BUT again) if I had to say that there was any time when I really said "enough," there were probably two incidents that were sobering enough for me to take it into consideration.

The first was the infected hole on the side of my hip. With my diabetes raging and me having the diet of a pig, it wasn't going to get better by itself. I was running a constant fever from the infection and went to get some antibiotics at the ER. They cleaned it up and when the doctor came in, he said I really fucked myself this time. He took a pencil out of his top pocket and inserted it into the hole, pushing the pencil in until three to four inches disappeared all the way into my leg. They had just done a CSCAN on me, and he said I had a "septic socket." That was a new one for me, right up there with MRSA, flesh-eating bacteria, and gangrene. The doctor said another half inch and it would have reached my hip bone, my bone would have gotten infected, and then I would have lost my leg.

I was still just thinking about which pain pills they would give me that I could sell and then get something that I could shoot that would make me not care. But before the doctors tore into me, cutting out the rest of the dead flesh and packing my hip with a couple feet of gauze, they made me sign a waiver that said if they were to go in and find it was already too far gone, I wouldn't object when they started hacking off pieces of my leg, even if they didn't stop until finally removing it at the hip. Then they made me sign the form that said I wouldn't be too upset if I was to die on them while they were doing the hacking. It really sucked to be conscious and not able to brush it off but instead have to stop and put serious thought into that horrifying scenario.

Then to have Mary come into my room before I went into the surgery and talk about funeral preparation, well that was not something I wanted to do. That was sobering, like I said. I knew a guy who had a big, rotten abscess on his arm and let the infection go and his arm turned black and they hacked it off at the elbow. He lived, he continued to shoot more dope, it wasn't the end of his world. It probably wouldn't be the end of my world, but the world would be better for me if I wasn't in a wheelchair. So this was my choice. I felt I ran as far as I could go. No more credit, no more money.

About a month before, right about the time when I moved in with Tom, I was digging through the remainder of my trash to see what I could try to barter for dope. I found a dollar bill ripped in half. Where had this come from? I had no idea. I guessed I must have found it somewhere. This was all the cash I had, maybe I had some loose change and a bus pass, but basically nothing. But that wasn't going to stop me. It was late at night and I wasn't going to go all night feeling like shit. I cut some pages out of a phone book to match the same size as three or four one-dollar bills, and I wrapped them inside the torn bill so all you could see was the green and went downtown on the bus. It was Sunday night and I took the second to last bus from Milwaukie into the city, so it was about 11:00 p.m.

I found the packs of drug dealers under the Burnside Bridge and on the stairwells, looking out for trouble. Here comes trouble. As I walked up to them, I zeroed in on one guy to deal with. At first, I was going to try to only get one bag, just take it and throw the fake money at the dealer and see what happens. But then I suddenly decided to ask for two bags. Desperation inspired boldness. I held the "money" down low and said, "Forty? Forty?" He looked around, looked at me, looked down at my hands, and then looked around again, all in the same motion. I said, "There are cops at the top of the stairs, be cool, man, c'mon." We both went kinda back and forth without exchanging anything, the vibe was most definitely not right. But he probably dealt with freaks trying to pull shit all the time, maybe this was the norm. Then I said, "Here, man, here, c'mon!" He put one big balloon, a forty, into my hand, and I stuffed the wad of fake paper into his so he could feel the real touch of the currency first.

I turned and headed for the stairs with my half gram of dope, and it took about three seconds for him to realize he had just been ripped off. I heard him say "hey!" and grab me by the shoulder. I spun around in one motion, pulling out this giant bone-handled hunting knife I took from a box of worthless crap in my house. Like the half-dollar bill, I had no idea where this giant hunting knife came from. I swung it hard and sliced at him from the top of his chest, across and down his stomach. I leaned in, picturing myself going completely through him. Fast and deep and I know it cut his coat open, I saw that. Maybe I cut his shirt and maybe whatever was beneath that. It was an old knife but it sliced. And I probably wouldn't have another chance to make this first impression. He jumped was posing as a recovering heroin addict because that was the Nirvana thing to do, and it was fashionable this month. I'm sure he had his struggles with whatever, but he just seemed full of shit. This guy was talking about how no matter how far gone he went into the abyss, he still had the support of his family and he always would pick up his trusty guitar and channel his pain through that. We busted out laughing. Everybody knows to become a scumbag junkie you have to burn down everything. Your family is one of the first to go, plus this guy still had a guitar!? We were throwing bricks through store windows to steal the tip jars off the counters. You have to let everyone go. There's no love, no loyalty or trust in this world that we choose. I was there. I'd burned everybody.

You know how local TV news will show surveillance footage of criminals caught in the act? It was getting common to be able to recognize "the most wanted" in the metro area. Often accused of grand larceny. They were people I slightly knew or would see around town, but some were even friends. Eventually, a former bandmate would be busted for armed robbery and head off to prison for seven years. He'd used a steak knife to rob a pharmacy. I wasn't shocked because I knew he was in bad shape. A couple of years earlier he tried to drive off with the van of a touring Scottish punk band. I think he might have been turning the key in the ignition when they caught him. It was a comical image but that degree of desperation isn't so funny. Other familiar faces would be nabbed for petty theft or more violent offenses, usually in pursuit of quick money to buy drugs. They did time in county lockup or federal prison. Maybe I could be "scared straight"? If I kept it up, it was only a matter of time before a closeup of my pitiful mug would appear on the screen. There was a reporter on one of the local channels who had been in the early punk scene. I could imagine him saying, as the footage aired, "Hey, I know that guy! Jerry?" As if I didn't already have enough motivation to make big changes.

Now I'm persona non grata with the rats of this city, and I want to get straight? What? How do I climb out? Ya know what? Fuck it. I was running out of excuses. I had jumped in, headfirst, I didn't care. Now maybe I can do the same thing to escape the pit. It's no secret what I did and who I am. I should admit it and try to clean this mess up. It can't get any worse. I should start with the one I burned the worst. Of all the people that I cut off and lied to and treated like shit, probably the one I loved the most, Mary, bore the biggest brunt of it. Although I never kicked in her door or stole her car, I took a couple years of her life. She started doing dope when she was with me and got strung out. Then I didn't want her to die with the rest of us, so I sent her home to get sober, but then shunned her and would have nothing to do with her. I would see her out and about, and she would be moving forward with her life and doing good. But I would look right past her. Ignore her. I was feeling sorry for myself and wound up choosing self-destruction. Maybe I thought if I treated her rotten, she would stay away and I wouldn't infect her.

But an infection was one of the things that reunited us. After my hip surgery, and I had tons of dressings on it, I had to care for it constantly. It required effort. I decided to fix this and let it heal properly. I gotta admit, this one spooked me. So that meant antibiotics and changing the dressings, keeping it clean, blah, blah. Even though I was still using all sorts of drugs and double-dipping on the methadone program, once I had my last big run, I started to slowly wean the other crap out of my life. Believe me, methadone is a big enough dragon to try to slay, ya don't need to be mixing more benzos and all the other stuff. It meant days of blackouts and rivers of slobber. Once I started actually pissing clean UAs and following the rules of the methadone program, I confessed to her and told her all the shit I had done. She had always been my friend since we were kids and she had gone through her own hell, she was just too smart to flush everything away. She saw some kind of future and she worked toward getting there. If I had thought it was too late for me to change when I was sixteen, what was I going to do now, twenty years later? I just started trying. You'll never know if you don't try or if you don't ask. Fuck, what have I got to lose? I asked for help.

I started piecing whatever parts I could salvage back together, and Mary had been used to patching me up before. She saved my blue-lipped ass more than once. I asked if it might be possible that she would help me take care of my latest surgery and see if we could let it heal properly. She gave me a set of rules. No needles, no drinking in front of her. No dope when I was around her. I was still squatting on Tom's floor, so I could go there and roll in the filth if I wanted to, and if I felt like pretending to be a citizen, I could hang out with Mary. I started seeing her more and more. I would stop by her house a couple days out of the week and she would patch me up, and then we'd hang out and watch television. As I said, she had recently moved in a direct line from Tom and his roommate's place in Milwaukie to downtown Portland. She was living in SE Portland. It wasn't too bad of a neighborhood. They still called it "Felony Flats," but it kind of varied street by street. There were a lot of methamphetamine users. With that comes crime. I guess it could be pretty sketchy.

One evening, I was over watching television and Mary heard a knock at the sliding glass door at the back of the house. I didn't hear anything, but she insisted someone was thumping around back there. I went to the back room and opened the curtains. There was a guy standing right outside the door, shirt off, drenched in sweat, pushing the glass door trying to knock it off its railing and pop the door out of the frame. I looked at him and he kept pushing. I knocked on the door loudly, and he looked me dead in the eye.

"Hey, what are you doing?" I shouted at him. His eyes were spinning in his sockets. He kind of focused on me for a few seconds and then went back to pushing on the door. Fuck, I thought. I'm gonna have to kill this fool. I knew he was completely spun, and I had been in this same position before. I had done this exact same thing and kicked a door off the hinges thinking it was someone else's house. I accepted that I should have been severely beaten for that. I really didn't want to have to beat this guy with a baseball bat or run him through with a knife, but you have to think, what's he going to do once he gets inside? I'm not a fan of involving the police, but this was a special case, and they would have to come anyway if I fucked the guy up. I called them as I stood at the window looking at him. He just kept trying to get in like a zombie; he really wasn't even there. I kept them on the line as they pulled up and tasered him a couple times (he was on meth) and then hauled him away.

Over the following weeks, I would come over and hang more and more, and one day it got to the point where I was begging her to let me move into her spare room. As I said, we have always been best friends, but after what we went through, she wasn't going to jump back into bed so quickly with this big work-in-progress. For me, I needed somewhere that felt comfortable, sane, and constant if I wanted to crawl out of the hellhole. You take on your surroundings like a chameleon. There was no way I could go anywhere but further down, if that was even possible, staying at that place with Tom. I love and appreciate Tom for giving me that place to hide, and I always will, but it was death there.

7

IF YOU'RE AROUND SOMETHING LONG enough, you get desensitized to it. I once knew a crazy family who lived next to the airport and they slept soundly as planes took off and landed a stone's throw away, shaking the house. People live next to a slaughterhouse and eat their morning breakfast with that pungent smell permeating their nose hairs. People work in morgues. Death camps. Killing fields. And drug addicts? Hey, hey, I'm not saying being strung out is the same as being a death camp guard, but you focus on other things besides freedom. Besides life.

After I moved out of Tom's place and started staying with Mary, I got some of my old stuff out of a storage shed, the stuff I had at the Foster Road apartment. Man, that stuff stank—a distinct odor that triggered a memory. But again, I'm not saying all people who are junkies stink. I can only speak for myself, and I most definitely had a sickly sweet odor that was hard to smell when I was rolling in it, but man, once I started to get my senses back, I noticed it. Those old dull senses. Gone yesterday, welcome back today. My senses all did come back—flooding back. Good sense? That would be debatable.

I went into Hooper Detox Center right before I moved outta Tom's and made a half-hearted attempt to quit dope for the fourteenth time. What they did there was monitoring with blood pressure medicines and then giving you a bunch of Stella', Thora', the Lith's and Lib's, I'm not really sure exactly what they were prescribing as I was whacked beyond comprehension and understanding, but the junkies all called them "dummy pills." Drool and slobber. I was completely numb from the neck up but after a couple days the rest of my body suddenly came back to life.

This was the old Hooper Detox Center on East Couch Street, when it was still coed, women here, men right here. They stopped doing that for obvious reasons but if you're on the street, strung out and really trying to get sober, you're not trying to cop a peek at some sick person in their underwear. I was on about day three, and my libido was rising from the dead. All I could do was lay in bed, completely stoned with spittle running down my face, but like I said, down below was ready to go out on the town. In a cloudy fog, I reached down and bumped against my crotch. An alarm sounded in my hospital-issued PJs. I grabbed my cock. It was like I hadn't felt it for months, a long-lost buddy. I started pulling on him as if to say, "Long fucking time, how ya been?" I jerked on it once and then twice and I remember looking over and seeing these people all just standing around and just staring down at me, wondering what the fuck I thought I was doing. I didn't care and I couldn't even be bothered. It was like Frankenstein's monster with fire. I just let out some animalist grunt and swatted at the air toward where these people were standing. "Eahhh! Go! Now!" I kept pulling until I nodded back off to sleep.

But the senses, when they came back, something like tasting orange juice was almost enough to make you orgasm. So I would smell, taste, feel. Hear? There was nothing I wanted to hear. I already thought I knew everything, and that is one of the reasons I wound up in this place. I didn't want to hear it, hear you, or hear them. You spend enough time not caring when you wake up next to a dead person that when you finally start to come around, you find yourself getting emotional and tearing up at a Pampers commercial. It felt good to be out of those woods. But I was far from reborn. Now I was honestly doing what I would consider "chipping," maybe once a week. I was still going over to Tom's new place. He had since left the place that I was staying at with him and moved about forty blocks directly east of where I was living with Mary. He was still sharing the space with the "1,000-yard stare" pedo.

Even though my life was changing, I still had a reputation that was hard to shed. Around this time a friend of mine from back East was thinking of moving to Portland. He had work in Southern California a few times a year and if he had time to spare, he'd come up here to hang out. Once, I decided to show him the town from end to end. We went all over, including a visit to Fred and Toody from Dead Moon at their Tombstone General Store in Clackamas. At the end of the day, we wound up in the Hawthorne District right before dusk. The plan was to visit a few cool shops and grab a bite to eat somewhere. As we were walking down the street to our first stop, I heard someone call out to me from fifty feet away. It was a guy in his early twenties putting up flyers and heavy-duty posters. He had a staple gun and a nail gun with him. "Hey, Jerry, you fucker, ya want some of this?" He made a big show of pointing the nail gun in my direction. I looked at this guy and I did not recognize him. He kept up a steady stream of curses. My friend and I kept on walking, but the hothead with the nail gun kept barking at me. I couldn't figure out where I could have crossed paths with this guy. After dinner, we walked back to where the guy had been putting up posters. I tore one down and took it home. I had never heard of them. The name sounded like some generic hodgepodge of vaguely alternative industrial punk metal. But I filed away the phone with this band's name on it, with instructions. When the caller mentioned his band, the young woman who answered the phone said, "You know, Jerry A. works here and he says someone from your band threatened him with a nail gun." The guy said, "Ah, well, ah, that was me. I didn't mean anything bad. It was a tribute. I like his band. I thought it was the most punk thing I could do." The Satyricon employee quickly said, "You can't threaten our staff. Your band is permanently banned from playing here." And then she hung up the phone. Ah, sweet justice. Tribute, huh? Imagine if he had worse motivations and more serious intentions.

But, yes, having a reputation means people may challenge you and you may not fully understand their reasons. It's like the last scene of *The Sopranos*. If Tony was whacked, maybe he never saw it coming. I didn't want to spend the rest of my days worried about angry guys wearing Members Only jackets walking up to me from behind, ready to pull the trigger, my world fading to black.

Before I forget, that bottle of Finnish liquor came to me in a roundabout way. My friend had been in Helsinki and wound up going out drinking with some of the leaders in the Finnish metal scene. The conversation got 'round to old Finnish punk bands like Terveet Kadet. Out of the blue, one guy mentioned that PI was one of his favorite bands. When my friend reported that he knew me, and would be seeing me in a month or two, the Finnish guy asked, "Does Jerry drink?" My friend just laughed. Then he related the story of me polishing off twenty-four complimentary bottles of Black Death vodka inside one week. The Finnish guy said, "Wow, *even to a Finn*, that is impressive! Okay, before you leave, I want to give you something to take to Jerry, with my compliments." When my friend came to visit me in Portland, he passed along the bottle of Koskenkorva and a bottle of something called Lonkero (which means "long drink"). The first was maybe vodka-based and the second was gin-based. Whatever, they went down my gullet before we boarded the bus to the venue downtown. (Yes, I took the bus to that gig. Remember when I told Wurzel from Motörhead that PI did not lead the lives of rock stars? I meant it.) Next came a fifth of vodka, which I had squirreled away. When I got to the venue, and drinks were "on the house," it was off to the races. I think the show went well, I got through it fine, people said it was a good set. I didn't rope in anyone with my mic cord and pull them up on the stage, but I did a trick or two with the mic stand, and I did my fire-breathing bit. But like Cinderella from hell, I went blotto soon after the clock struck midnight.

That marked the first time my visitor had really seen how much I could drink. It must have been eye-opening. I think I was drinking to get loose onstage. I was still battling drug addiction at the time. It was a hard battle to win. Though I was wanting to quit, I wound up dialing the dealer most days. That week, my guest and I would have conversations at the kitchen table two or three times a day while I was lighting my crack pipe. Once I said, "I'm really glad you don't do drugs—and that you aren't an addict." He playfully shot back through the second-hand smoke, "Well, we spend so much time at this table that it feels like I am!" It was a funny line and my joking response was straight outta The Three Stooges, "Why, I oughta...!" But I was starting to make real attempts at quitting.

A couple of days after the DK's show, we were walking in my neighborhood. I had a small slip of paper (Post-it size) with the number of my new dealer (Bobby must have been in jail and this was the number for the stand-in during his time in the joint). I said, "This is the only number I have for my dealer, and I'm so serious about quitting that I'm tearing this up right now so I won't have access. I won't be so tempted." I tore it up into four pieces and threw them on the ground in front of a neighbor's house. I was determined. Everything was fine—for a few hours. The next day would find me down on my hands and knees at sun-up, desperate for those tiny bits of paper littering the neighbor's lawn. I found them and taped everything back together and immediately called my dealer. It would be quite some time before I was totally off hard drugs, but I was seriously trying.

The next time my friend passed through was on the eve of a European tour. We were tooling around downtown one afternoon and decided to take the bus to visit Tom. I was skint and had to pool all my change for the fare. As I was feeding nickels and dimes into the box, a teenage boy on the bus was looking right at me, smirking and rolling his eyes. He must have been about seventeen, and I pegged him as someone who might have been into goth or emo. He was probably thinking, "Why is this penniless fat fool taking so long? Is this guy a wino?" As I walked past him to the back of the bus, he had a look of disgust on his face. My friend took a seat right across from this kid. A few stops later, one of the kid's buddies, another teenage boy, got on the bus and sat down with him. He had spotted me and said to the kid, "Dude, Jerry A. from Poison Idea is on the bus!" The kid was super excited: "Really? Are you sure? Where?" Apparently, he was a big fan of our band. When his friend told him to look back and he realized it was me, the look on his face was priceless. He had no idea.

That day I probably had three dollars in change in my pocket. That's all I had on me and I didn't have much more to my name. When we exited the bus, I went to the convenience store near Tom's and barely had enough for a bottle of water. The clerk would not have believed that a few days later I'd be performing in front of thousands of people at a big festival in Europe. That I'd soon be enjoying the sights of Paris or would have hundreds of Londoners singing along to a song I had written. And there's the other side of the equation: someone who had been singing along to "Just to Get Away" at one of those European concerts might be puzzled why I would be struggling again for bus fare in Portland the following month.

By the way, I would eventually get to meet my Finnish booze benefactor. His name was Ewo, and he was a music promoter. He was a strapping blond Viking giant and he flew in to see PI play Oslo, Norway, during one of the Euro tours where we didn't make it to Finland. I hope it occurred to me at the time that he was the one who had sent me the drinks. Those bottles made it halfway around the world and I had pounded them down in thirty seconds, without stopping to appreciate the taste. At the very least, I hope I thanked him and said, "Cheers!"

8

I HAD MY HOUSE RULES at the new place with Mary, so if I wanted to get loaded, I would sneak over to Tom's. Mary was still sober and never went back to even having as much as a single drink. That first run with me and the tour of Europe with Gift was enough to make her never want to experience it again. I had gotten bored stumbling around out of it, and though it took a couple of years, I was slowly cleaning myself up. I wasn't getting fucked up every day, and now I was putting more time back into the band. We were still a bunch of fuckups but we had recently done another recording and Tom played guitar on it. When that happened, we were supposed to tour Europe again to promote the record. I then faced the old problem of being on methadone and trying to tour out of the country for a month. I'd done this so many times by now I knew what to do, but it was all a big hassle. If I had ever thought of this as an adventure, trying to score dope in every strange city or smuggling a half ounce of dope into whatever country, I now saw it as a deterrent. A roadblock. Things would have run a lot smoother and the shows would have gone a lot better if I just decided to stop using.

Poison Idea was ripping these people off; it wasn't the same as when we started. Now we were just playing for dope. There was no way on earth that Tom could have toured with us at this point.

He knew and understood this as well as anyone and was resigned to it, and we had to accept that fact. No matter how much we would have liked him to go with us, it was hard enough for me to make it on the road without having to worry about Tom.

We once had a guy in the band who didn't last long. He was a good player but his drug addiction was so strong that when we'd pick him up at Satyricon to go practice, we'd first have to give him a ride to his dealer so he could cop. Then he might want to go to McDonald's so he could shoot up in the bathroom and grab a burger. That wasn't gonna work. It only took two or three practices to know this would be a giant headache. I needed this like I needed a sharpened stone in my shoe. So we kicked this guy out before he really started. He was around for a cup of coffee—I don't think he lasted a week. And now Tom had become like that guy—he required that level of high maintenance.

Then the rest of the guys started going through the same hurdles. Tom would stay home while the rest of us would go on tour. The show must go on! There were plenty of little episodes and big decisions that I had to deal with as the band leader. Though, trust me, I do realize the band's not all about me. Everyone in the group, along with the road crew, is important. People have their own issues and emotional baggage. Guys could be preoccupied with concerns back home, like a budding relationship or a pending court case. Or something unexpected could come up on the road, like a bad case of Montezuma's revenge or getting bottled onstage. No matter what, we'd all have to soldier on. This was our day job.

Lemme just give one story, which might give a taste of the decisions I have faced. We did a series of shows in Texas, and then finished up with a gig in New Orleans. I don't remember many details about the shows, though I think we played with Verbal Abuse on that short tour. And that might have been the first time I went to Corpus Christi, a city I liked the look of. Anyway, the day after the New Orleans show, when the band was to assemble and head to the airport for the flight home to Portland, one member was nowhere to be found. He had left the venue and had never returned to our hotel. Now it was time to leave. We had his luggage, his gear, his tour money, and I think we even had his ID. All we knew was that he had left the club to head into maybe the roughest ward of the city in search of drugs.

So we waited for him. We kept saying. "Let's give him five more minutes" until we didn't have five more minutes to give. Did he OD; did he get shot; did he hook up with some girl; did he get lost? We had no idea. We knew it would be hard on him to be stranded there with no money or ID. We were reluctant to leave him, but it was time to go. We had absolutely waited as long as we could. At this point, we'd have to rush to make our flight. Finally, I made the hard call: "Let's go. He's a grown-up. He'll figure it out."

Right then, here he comes, just in the nick of time. Another minute or two and we'd have left without him. He sure had a wild story to tell. It turns out he had gone to a crack house and then heard music coming out of a nearby party down the road. Who knows what possessed him, but he didn't think twice, he just wandered in. Folks were getting high and dancing and he joined in without saying a word, like he belonged. He was the only white person there and being dressed in punk attire also made him stand out. The people wanted to know who he was and why he was there. He just innocently stated his full name and said he was "from Portland, Oregon." For whatever reason, they let him stay. Maybe they thought he was a rube or fearless or crazy or harmless. They didn't bounce him out or rough him up. Instead, they thought he was genuine and cool and even made him an honorary member.

He spent the rest of the night dancing, getting loaded, having a good time, and partying until dawn with gangsters in the hood.

We were able to make the flight home, barely. Later, I got to wondering what would have happened had he gotten stranded there. Would he have stayed on the streets and slept on park benches? Or crashed with some of his new "friends" from the party? Maybe he'd have called me to wire him the bus fare home. He couldn't have flown without ID, but he could have taken the bus. I could have bought his ticket in advance, which he could have claimed by answering a security question at the station in New Orleans. Or I could have sent his tour money via Western Union. Maybe he'd have tried to earn the money himself by working as a dishwasher or some other menial job. The reason I still think about this is that Hurricane Katrina happened soon after, and if he had been stuck down there, how would it have turned out?

It's hard making decisions for the band, but, hey, even a broken clock is right twice a day! The band would work and sweat our asses off on the road for a month and when we'd come back, I felt I had to give Tom a taste of the money we made. Like paying your tribute to the mafia boss. I'd tell him that people would ask about him and send their regards. A lot of people had heard that he was dead and when they heard he was still alive, they would get all misty-eyed and tell us to send their love back to him. Then Tom would get all choked up hearing that people cared enough about him to send their regards.

9

OF ALL THE PEOPLE IN my life, besides Mary, I had probably spent more overall time with Tom. When I was younger and we'd just started the band, I would hang out with Tom for weeks and months on end while I was still living in Glenn's mother's basement. Later, when I started living with Mary, the two of us would go over a couple of times a week and hang out with him and party. Or we would pick him up and take him to one of the Oregon beaches around Gearhart. We spent a lot of time on the Washington side of the Columbia River Gorge—he loved it there—plus local places like Sauvie Island that were convenient. There was a time when we were best friends. Then when Tom and I were both going through our own separate addictions, we each ran with our own pack of thieves. I didn't see him a lot then, but we kept in contact. Now that I was somewhat stabilized again, I was seeing him almost every day.

I was going to the same methadone clinic as Tom at first. He would usually take the bus and time it so he would get there just as they were closing for the day. But as I started hanging out with him more, we started going down there together. I would go to the clinic first thing in the morning. I had my worker's papers, so I could go there and take care of my business and get the fuck out and not have to hang out and mingle with the riffraff. I started picking up Tom every morning, about 5:30 a.m. Some days we'd get breakfast, some days I'd just drop him off. Occasionally, we would both do our biz and then go back and hang out for an hour or so and bullshit. I had to get the car back home so Mary could go to work, but she would let me pick up Tom and use it in the morning. He always made an effort to get up and get his shit together to get out of the house on time. I mean, a free ride to the methadone clinic and back. Wow, what a deal!

I was happy to be hanging out with my friend, and he seemed like he might possibly consider eventually playing more shows with us. Depending on the day and the mood, things were looking up. Like I said, we'd just recorded a new record, *Latest Will and Testament*. And he had been happy with how it turned out. We would talk all the time, that's all we had. I would give him my take on the situation, how I was tired of running like this and thought we could pull ourselves out of this pit and start over again. But now it was Tom's turn to think that it was too late. He couldn't see my plans for the next big thing. No matter what solution I would throw at him, he'd shoot it down. We would argue for days about this. When he was by himself, he would write down his thoughts and opinions in notebooks. I can still picture his handwriting. He would often write sitting up in bed, in which case it was a big scrawl. When I read through these journals, I realized his problems were more severe than I thought. I was depressed, then I was optimistic. Tom was depressed, then he was more depressed. I can't say for certain that Tom wanted to die, but I can say that I know he didn't want to live.

One day, I got up and drove over to give him his morning ride. He didn't look too healthy on this particular morning. Tom got in the car and even though he had just taken a shower and was wearing relatively clean clothes, the smell of urine was pouring out of his skin. I told him he smelled like a wino and that he stunk. He said his piss had been really dark and he was afraid his kidneys were giving out. I wasn't surprised considering the shit malt liquor he liked to drink. If someone was going to go to the store for him and they were buying, he would still get whatever crap had the highest alcohol content. That was the deciding factor. Rotgut. This wasn't even beer, they couldn't call it beer by law because it wasn't fermented and made with hops and grains like beer. This was chemicals poured into a vat. Swill. It tasted like cologne to me.

At one time in my life, when I was young, I drank Olde English 800 and I kind of learned to enjoy the taste, as plastic as it was. But these brands that Tom was drinking were just horrible, rotten, bum juice. Tom would drink this crap like water and his kidneys and liver wouldn't even process it. His piss would come right out of his pores. And I know it's not always easy for morbidly obese people to wash every inch of their bodies, especially if they have flaps and folds. I really didn't care that he stunk. Tom was my best friend and best friends overlook stupid small things like stinking or having bad breath, but when I said something about his smell, he got upset. He kept apologizing. I kept telling him it didn't matter, I was just worried about why that was happening and that we should make a doctor's appointment to see what's going on. I didn't care how he looked, what he said, or what he did. I had his back, always. I'd lived with Tom on occasion, and had been close friends with him for twenty-five years. I knew his habits and they didn't faze me.

I would tell him that I wished he would try to make some plans for the future, but he would cut me off and remind me how weak caring about someone sounds. For me to show any kind of empathy was leaving my throat exposed. He was a sensitive person, but he tried to be the tough guy. We went to the clinic that morning and did our thing. Then I drove him back home and asked what he had planned for the rest of the day. He was going to do his usual and would I give him a ride at the same time tomorrow? Of course. Later that night he called me, and he asked if I would be over at five thirty. Yes, I said. He then said, "I washed my clothes." "What?" I asked. I had already forgotten about that morning. "I washed my clothes and took a shower, I don't smell." "Jesus, Tom, I don't care. I fucking told you that. Now who's being sensitive?" Even though I brought him back to the scuzzy level of jocularity that we shared as friends, I felt bad; he sounded sheepish. I didn't care that he smelled a little and I was sorry I said anything.

The next morning, I got up and went over and knocked on his side window so as to not wake up his roomie. He didn't answer the door. I tapped again and then figured he either went back to sleep or someone maybe had already given him a lift after an all-night crack and smack binge. I went to the clinic by myself, dosed, and went back home. I asked Mary if I could drive her to work and borrow her car, in case I needed to run around that day. I drove her to work and walked back into the house to the phone ringing. It was Tom's roommate. "I think something's wrong with Tom." I asked what he meant. The roommate said he was just lying there and not moving. I asked, "How long has he been like that?" He said a couple of hours. I asked if he called an ambulance. No. "Call 9-1-1 right now, I'm on my way!"

I beat the ambulance there but not the police. The cops had already pulled up, and they found Tom dead. They ran a check on his roommate, who had outstanding warrants for his arrest, and had him handcuffed in the back of the police car. They asked me for my ID, ran a check on me (since this house was a known drug user hangout), and I was clean. Then I told them I'd wait there for the coroner, and they said it might be a while. The one police officer rolled out with Tom's roomie in the back of his car and I was left there with Tom. I sat in the room and wondered what had happened. I wasn't there, but I knew that everything he was always afraid of happening had happened. Something went wrong and he was stuck here with that guy, the guy who always panicked. The guy that Tom warned me about over the years, saying many times, "I just hope nothing ever goes down when I'm alone with him." Well, he had reason to worry. The guy said he found him earlier. A couple of hours? I don't even want to think about it.

I only talked to that guy a couple times after that day. He told me that he took some dope out of Tom's pockets when he found him, so Tom wouldn't be blamed. Blamed? He rifled through a dead friend's pockets and stole his shit. I packed up Tom's ID, his personal notebooks where he jotted down his thoughts, and his busted-up Epiphone guitar. His first guitar. I took all these things home with me. I still have all that stuff. I wonder if the creep still has the dope. So then I just sat there with my dear old friend asking him questions that I knew I'd never get answers to. I honestly looked up into the corner of the room, above where Tom was, to see if there was a sign. People who have near-death experiences report they leave their body and can remember looking down at the room. I was looking for any sign from the other side, even a rustling of the curtain. I didn't see nothin'. Well, I guess people are still hoping Houdini will get in touch. After a few minutes, I called my bass player, Chris, and told him what had happened. He said he'd come right over.

It took a while for the coroner to show up and they wound up calling a couple of extra people. The reason for this was that Tom was so big, probably somewhere between 450–500 pounds, that they needed more help lifting him up. I just sat back and watched. The first time one of them said something about the trash around the room, or the syringes or whatever, I made it clear that they needed to do their fucking job and keep their mouths shut or there were going to be more body bags leaving the room that day. Then he was gone. I called the boys (the dealers, not the band) and they came over, asked where everyone was. I said Tom was dead and the other guy was in jail. They got spooked and quickly sold me what I wanted and zipped out of there. I fixed and passed out on Tom's bed. Then our bass player came over and woke me up and I told him what I thought had happened. I'll never know for sure, I wasn't there when it actually happened, but I was there an hour or two afterward. Whatever happened, it wasn't good. This is how it all ends. Just the end.

I had to find Tom's sister's phone number and call her to tell her that her brother had died. I told her all the things that he had always told me about what he wanted done. Some stuff like that we talked about for years, to make sure the other person was able to honor our wishes, when the first of us died. All that stuff could go straight out the window once he was gone, since family members often make their own decisions. His family didn't know what he wanted, but I did and I passed along the message. Tom had told me he wanted to disappear as soon as he died. He didn't want to stick around. They got rid of him fast. They cremated him and spread his ashes over a lake he used to love swimming in when he was a kid. A year or two later that lake dried up, most likely from climate change. It took me a long time to accept that he was gone.

One thing that would have meant something to him was that *The New York Times* ran an obituary. Maybe a week after Tom died, I got a call from an author who wanted to write something about Tom. A friend of mine from the East Coast happened to be visiting me that day, so I put the phone down for a second to ask if he knew of a writer by the name of Kelefa Sanneh. He said, yeah, he's a culture critic for the *New York Times* and sometimes writes for *The New Yorker*. So it was legit, and I had a long conversation with the writer. By this point, there had already been a funeral/memorial, but since we were an underground band it took time for word to spread. I know Tom would have been honored and proud. He never could have imagined that he would make the obit page of the *Times*.

Probably the biggest thing for me to get used to (besides not seeing him or just hearing the sound of his voice) was not being able to pick up the phone and call him with a question about music. He was a walking encyclopedia of rock music, and he was a thinking man. I called this guy every day when he was alive. I found myself picking up the phone for a couple of months and then catching myself. "Oh, yeah, shit." That ain't gonna happen again. I'd like to say that he died quietly in his sleep, while dreaming of riding his dirt bike and jumping over some ramps. And fuck, why not? That's why I'm putting all this down, so the truth will be left behind. So, I'll rewrite this small bit of truth and say that he *did* pass peacefully in his sleep. Just between you and I. Bullshit.

10

When I began writing this memoir, I made the decision that it should cover my life up until Tom died. It was kind of arbitrary, but it seemed fitting. That was the end of a major chapter in my life. Even though I have hundreds of other stories from my early years, some pretty extreme and unique, if I were to write another book, I might pick it up after Tom's funeral. Trust me, there's enough material for a handful of books and screenplays. In fact, right now there's an intense situation going on in my life that I'm struggling with and don't know how it will turn out. It feels like the past six months could be a whole book.

But there are things I can mention without going into great detail. For one thing, the band would continue. I guess a lot of people thought we wouldn't go on without Tom. Well, it was difficult to carry on without Tom, but it had happened before. When he quit the band on that European tour, it really hurt me. At the time, I just threw my hands up in the air and ended the band. But after Tom got some rest, he decided he missed playing. He started other projects and then we reformed Poison Idea. But his involvement with the band would come and go over the years. He'd write songs, he'd record, he'd play local shows, he'd do interviews and photo shoots. But he wouldn't do much touring.

At his size, and with his substance and health issues, Tom wasn't built for touring. On the road, Tom could be my best friend and my worst enemy. On those last major tours, he had to be accommodated. It felt like he had to be waited on constantly. For instance, if we stayed in a motel, he wanted to be on the ground floor. He didn't want to have to climb stairs. If we did a photo shoot, we might have to delay it for him to score drugs. Maybe we were running late to record but we'd first have to stop for him to get food. After we reformed the band, he rarely made long trips. He did make the day-long drive to SF once or twice. Did he go with us to Austin? He did fly to Newark in 2002, when we played CBs and made a short tour of NE cities. That's about it. We'd have to get a fill-in for him on tours. Tom and I were both big guys with drug habits, but I always sucked it up and put the band first. I was determined to soldier on.

Not long ago, I posted a flyer from a show The Imperialist Pigs and Poison Idea did together in the early days. People wrote in, impressed that Tom had done double duty that night. Well, he hadn't. The Imperialist Pigs was Tom's band and Poison Idea was my band. PI was lucky enough to nick him later on, and we were suddenly much better when we joined forces. But, through the years, I'm the only constant member of the band. I write the words and a lot of the music. The band existed before Tom, it existed after he quit or would take breaks from playing live, and the band would exist after Tom passed away. He would have wanted and expected me to carry on.

It's been more than a decade now since Tom passed away, and I realize I'll always miss him. Tom briefly had a radio show on KBOO in the eighties. I think it was on "The Autonomy Hour." I recently found a clip and played it on my podcast. Many people contacted me to say one of two things: if they didn't know him and had never heard him speak, they were surprised by his voice—it was different from what they had imagined. Or if they had known Tom, they said how great it was to hear his voice again.

I always regarded Tom as sort of "the Orson Welles of punk rock." It wasn't just because of his large size and his beard. He was smart, learned, playful, talented, and a true raconteur.

Tom was a good conversationalist. It helped that he was extremely well-read. He could talk in depth about Burroughs, Bukowski, Selby, Céline, Bierce, Twain, Shakespeare, and many others. Plus, he had an encyclopedic knowledge of rock music and loads of good stories. If you spent a couple of hours with him, he might discuss, say, a Hawkwind rarity or the latest Motörhead album, something James Baldwin had written about Jean Genet, national politics, underground comics, nineteenth century Russian novels, sixties girl groups, the criminal justice system, a forgotten sitcom from his childhood, British vs. Japanese grindcore, the Dutch band Larm, an old hit by The Flamin' Groovies, the current deal at his favorite Chinese buffet, a phone call he had made to Quentin Crisp (whose phone number was listed in the NYC telephone directory), seventies exploitation movies, a Lord Buckley line, how a Richard Pryor routine reminded him of both Lenny Bruce and Iceberg Slim, how easy it was to be brainwashed by consumer culture, an anecdote from an Ed Bunker memoir, a funny riff he'd made on his ham radio, his beloved Fix "Vengeance" single, *A Confederacy of Dunces*, an early album by Outkast, lines from *The Tube Bar* recordings, novels by John Fante, guitar solos by the Allman Brothers contrasted with an obscure European prog band, text he wanted to use for an upcoming concert flyer or record ad, rare albums on John Fahey's Takoma Records label, how sad it was that sports were valued over intellect in our society, plus a few sordid stories from the street. The next time would be totally different with equally varied subject matter. I especially enjoyed his funny anecdotes. Tom could weave a story about some crazy incident he'd witnessed on the bus ride back from the clinic that would keep me in stitches for days.

Tom was my comrade for over twenty-five years. After spending so much time with him and sharing so many of the same interests and reference points, it was like we had our own shorthand and occupied the same wavelength. One time we answered an interviewer's questions entirely with Bukowski quotes. It was a fun exercise for us, though I'm not sure if the journalist ever picked up on it. I can say it cracked *us* up.

Tom was my best friend for many years. I saw him at his best and I saw him at his worst. He was my closest songwriting partner, and I wish we could have played music together forever. But life goes on.

11

One thing that has changed dramatically in the years since Tom's death is Portland itself. The city has become a boom town. We have more hipsters, more homeless, and some governmental policies that aren't working in a city that gets more expensive by the day.

There's a housing crisis and the streets are full of homeless encampments. The problem is epidemic. In many cities, most homeless people have shelter at night. In Portland, a large percentage are unsheltered. Don't take my word for it, look into it, compare Portland to other major cities. The homeless and drug situation might be even more dire in Seattle. A great number of the homeless in Portland are tweakers. When I was growing up, most bums were alkies; now, most are drug addicts. I'm more understanding of certain homeless communities (including runaways, war veterans with PTSD, families, people with mental illness, individuals who fell on hard times and are genuinely trying to get back on their feet) than people who just get high, commit petty crimes, and take up an outsized share of social services. Occupy Portland started with good intentions. People arrived with genuine political concerns, but then the homeless came in looking for a place to camp and it turned into something else. I knew someone who helped clean it up and he said it was a shitty mud pit that reeked, and there were discarded syringes everywhere. A trash heap. There were reports of serious crimes within the camp and that's more alarming than the stench. Maybe it was an easy place to blend in for a few wolves in sheep's clothing.

Sometimes, it seems like tweakers are given keys to the city. There are some stories that are so outlandish that it can seem like a segment of the homeless population is holding the city hostage. Imagine an old lady who lives on your block. One day she comes home and finds a group of homeless people camped out in her yard, and they are blocking direct access from her car to her front door. She is scared and the police are called. They tell the homeless they have to go and give them a certain amount of time to disband. The police leave. The homeless take their time to gather their possessions and simply move across the street to another property. Again, the police are called, and they come back and tell them to move along. Okay, okay, they say. What do they do? They move back in front of the old lady's house. For the police, it must seem like a game of whack-a-mole. I'm not at all about politics. I'm just observing and reporting what I see. It's minor irritations like tweakers going into residential neighborhoods and rummaging through recycling and making a mess. Or more serious behavior like sleeping in the doorways of businesses and scaring off customers. I know it's not an easy situation; it just seems like nothing is working. There are a lot of other problems, and there could always be a catastrophic emergency like a tsunami or a contagion. Something that could kill a bunch of us but isn't our end. Where day-to-day life is put on hold and there is a lot of anxiety, panic, and uncertainty. We would have to meet the moment. But the homeless situation needs to be addressed, and I know that well-done is better than well-said. It needs to be on a front burner.

I recently saw a homeless tweaker that I know sitting on the street downtown. He's not the stereotype of the harmless guy spouting nonsense, talking to the wind. This dude is a bad guy who had been in jail for horrendous acts. I'll spare you the details. Think "heinous." Some sympathetic people saw him and asked if there was anything they could get for him. He said, "I could use bottles of water because I get so thirsty." The good Samaritans came back with a twenty-four-pack of water, feeling proud of their good deed. As soon as they were out of sight, the guy started opening the bottles and pouring them out. He took the empty bottles in to redeem. He got two dollars and forty cents from that charade and he was well on his way to another cheap bag of dope.

There was a time when I was homeless. I was an addict and an alcoholic who did what those people tend to do: lie, cheat, and steal. But the thing is, I didn't want any help. I wanted to shoot drugs. I only wanted to get loaded. I had nothing to live for and I didn't care if I lived or died. I only wanted to get high and stay high. Nothing else mattered. This is true for many of the homeless in Portland but many "experts" don't acknowledge it. That's not all that I see but I do see that.

A friend of mine told me that city officials at a town hall meeting were saying how graffiti is good because it is a form of creative expression. They were trying to rationalize it after there were a series of complaints. Hey, I'm all for self-expression. But when someone complained that the homeless were tagging her neighborhood with "88" (a white nationalist symbol celebrating Hitler), the council sat stunned. One of them finally said "they would not do that." I understand why freedom of speech is important and I do remember when the ACLU lost members after defending the rights of neo-Nazis to march in Skokie, even though they were appalled by the ideology being expressed. But in this case, it was more than just hate speech, it was also defacing private property. How can that be justified and excused? It seems like the perpetrators were getting a pass because they were homeless. People complain about white men being privileged and entitled, but most homeless tweakers are white men and it seems like they get the benefit of the doubt. Maybe the council members are well-intentioned, but some may be out of touch. You can be compassionate and still disagree with policies of the city council. I'm relating this story as someone who wrote a song against racism called "Discontent" that called out Nazis and also released a press statement condemning them.

From my perspective, the local PD is better now than it was. Okay, maybe the bar wasn't set very high. There is room for improvement, yet, in my experience, cops have gotten a little easier to deal with here. Part of it may be that I'm no longer a junkie running with criminals, so I don't get hassled the way I used to. But it definitely seems like there's more transparency than in the past. Nationwide, there are notorious hot spots for police corruption and brutality, yet it doesn't seem like Portland is one of those places. I was a fan of the TV series *The Shield* about rogue cops in LA. Some storylines reminded me of old events in Portland, but I think cops are watched more closely today. I'm sure there are few bad seeds and things can get swept under the rug. Throughout the country, cell phones and surveillance cameras and media scrutiny have shined a light on human rights being ignored or abused. Watershed moments have led to awakenings and reform. Some good things came about as Portland became a liberal bastion and some bad things too. There are still inequalities and systemic issues like poverty and racism that need structural change. Extremist groups clash in the streets. I haven't written about that because it's ongoing and may escalate, and this is not a blog. Then there is the growing population of homeless people. Things are far from perfect. Hopefully there will be positive change. Not all change is progress; it could also mean going backward. I mean, is auto-tune progress? What will this place be like in twenty-five years? I suppose we help create the future by the choices and contributions we make today.

I've gotten to know a few cops in recent years and there are times I feel for what they go through with the public. You know, all cops are bastards until a homeless guy is shitting on your lawn or a tweaker is trying to break into your house.

During the course of writing this book, drugs have gotten dirt cheap in this town and the quality is really pure. You can get a bag of dope for seven dollars. There was a time when a cup of coffee cost a buck while a bag of dope was twenty dollars. A little light panhandling or recycling bottles can yield seven bucks. The other day I saw a guy shooting up on the sidewalk in broad daylight, just a few feet from the curb. I used to see guys tasered over less. But it's not deemed to be a violent crime, so now the police might not even bother with it. If they made an arrest, the guy could get bounced before the cops even finish writing up the paperwork. In a way, drugs have been decriminalized. I suppose I picked a bad time to quit. Now a cup of coffee at a gourmet coffee shop can actually cost more than a bag of dope. What would the old guard (RIP) think of that?

Local government seems out of touch, and town meetings can get pretty heated. Speakers get shouted down. That's gotta be frustrating. I know politics is often about horse-trading. But for positive transformation, there should be open communication. Portland has become an expensive place to live. It had been a cheap place until transplants started arriving in droves from California and hotbeds like Brooklyn and Austin. It feels like some of these people are locusts who swoop in and take what they can from the city and suck it dry before moving on to another spot on the hipster trail. But where do people go who are priced out? I'd guess Vancouver and other parts of Southern Washington, maybe Eugene. I wonder if any move East to reeling cities like Cleveland and Detroit, where their dollars can go further.

I wonder what Tom would make of how the town has changed. What would he think of all the trendy young guys who look like updated versions of Sam Elliott in Westerns, with the big difference being that they are the exact opposite of rugged, self-sufficient, independent heroes? Tom would probably laugh at the pose and call them candy asses. It's a trend that can't go away fast enough.

The town has gone overboard in political correctness. Sometimes it seems like we're living a *SNL* parody. One thing's for sure, it would be the kiss of death for a business to be *perceived* as being politically incorrect. I've had visitors from pretty enlightened places around the world who scratch their heads in hyper-sensitive Portland. A feminist from Berlin told me she didn't know what to make of all the rules, which she found ridiculous. A world traveler told me it was like being in a straitjacket surrounded by land mines. Maybe it will get more extreme or maybe the pendulum will swing back in the other direction. As an artist, I don't like having shackles put on the language I use. The extremes in PC stuff can get me down. I was on my way to a Morrissey concert a couple of years ago when I made some innocent comment that a woman I was with misconstrued. She had to work hard to be offended; it took crazy mental gymnastics. She took offense where none was intended. Then she started loudly complaining about "mansplaining" and "power to the patriarchy." Now, I had been looking forward to this concert for months, and I might have gotten my ticket the day the show went on sale, but her comments bugged me so much I couldn't enjoy any of the show. It ruined it for me. Recently, I went to a Brian Wilson concert where a tweaker stood up and started singing along out of key at the top of his lungs. Even though he was ruining the concert for everyone, no one would say anything because it's considered being insensitive to his condition. I wound up leaving the concert after a few songs. That's the way the city has turned.

You see a nude woman in the middle of a busy downtown street digging through trash and then start scrubbing her ass with nothing but a small hand towel. Without a care in the world. And you think, "Now I've seen everything." But then a few blocks later you watch a legless guy scoop up dog poop with his hands and smear the most offensive hate symbols on a nearby wall while shouting utter madness. Just when you thought you had seen everything. Hieronymus Bosch could have gotten ideas for a painting of hell.

Portland has become a city of transplants. I see fewer old people as the place becomes the next stop on the yipster trail. When I go to shows, I seldom recognize anybody. Sure, part of it is the natural progression that people tend to stop going out as often as they get older, but it just feels like a different place now. The city is better in some ways than it used to be. There's more ethnic diversity, better food options, an inexpensive light rail that moves people around town, an airport that has been named best in the nation, more entertainment options. Yeah, I still remember the early days when Portland was a "one cool show per night" town. But I'm starting to think I wouldn't be sad to leave.

Old Portland is disappearing. Cool buildings are being sold to developers. They tear down these historic buildings and rip the spirit and soul out of the city. These leveled buildings are about people on the take getting paid. Sometimes, I wonder if politicians and developers are playing a long game setting up specific neighborhoods to fail, which in turn leads to gentrification. Or maybe they don't think about the long game. There are just greedy bastards, with no forethought, just going for the quick-and-run. And then flat-out lie, figuring they don't need to be accountable. They won't be around ten years later to be held responsible...they're like carpetbaggers. Like they say on *The Wire*, you gotta follow the money.

There's a cycle I've seen time and again. A building goes tits up. Then it gets vandalized, maybe graffitied. The homeless come in. Then the city gets rid of the homeless. Food trucks come in. Then things are rezoned. The property people come in, and then the building gets leveled. At which point, you know condos may be coming in. And finally, some soulless, multi-unit, cookie-cutter box goes up.

I suppose some things are slow to change. The police response time is faster for wealthy neighborhoods than poor neighborhoods. And Eighty-Second still remains sketchy, no matter what they try or however they attempt to rebrand it.

When I talk about Portland today, it might sound like sour grapes. Acknowledging problems is a step toward solving them. There's a lot of work to be done to move in a positive direction. I started thinking about it and wrote many pages, but I threw them away because I didn't want to start editorializing and have people say, "What's Jerry going on about now?"

I do worry about the censoring of ideas. It's dangerous to start banning art we don't agree with. Who gets to make that decision? Where would that end? A bland world.

Maybe Tom checked out at a good time. He would have hated all the fake news, propaganda, escalating culture wars, and politicians drawing battle lines to create division. And that's where we're at. He wouldn't have had time for that. Peace!!!! Goddamn it!!!!!

Portland was a Podunk, backwater town to Tom. He grew up here, dreaming of more options. For a kid like me, arriving wide-eyed from a small Montana town, it was a metropolis full of almost limitless possibilities.

The neighborhood that Tom was living in when he breathed his last is currently being raped by developers. It's like the death star when they come in. It's also common for developers to scoop up a property without ever intending to do anything with it. They just flip it to other developers. It's a quick cash grab. I can imagine ugly empty blocks and cookie-cutter strip malls. Woody Guthrie had lived in a rooming house in Lents, just a block from where Tom died. Apparently Woody did not like Portland much. He was only around for a month or so, but he was very productive. He wrote around thirty songs, some of which are considered classics. But I also think his marriage busted up when he was here, so he was probably glad to beat it out of town. No love lost. I think there's a movement to preserve the house as an historic site and put up a plaque. But I wonder what Woody Guthrie would think of all the commercialization and gentrification that is taking place in Portland. I think he'd be rolling over in his grave. Didn't he once sing something about bankers robbing you with a fountain pen?

12

I'LL SAY THIS ONE TIME, this ain't the end of the story. This isn't the whole story. And again, this is only my version of it.

When Tom passed, all of a sudden people were talking about, "I remember that time when I walked in on him at the bathroom at Satyricon and he had a rig in his arm, and he pulled it out and said, 'Ya want some?' and then he just popped it back in his arm and continued to shoot up." I wasn't there for that but I can tell you that never happened. There's so many inconsistencies in that sentence. It's all complete crap and yet everybody swears on a stack of MRRs that it happened. Maybe in their age-addled dream it is a reality. But I'm saying this now, setting the record straight, so when I'm gone if someone is looking for what really happened they can use this for reference. Oftentimes, what becomes the official history is anything but—it's full of clichés and errors that are passed down and accepted as gospel by people who weren't there to experience it firsthand.

Sure, there are at least two sides to every story. A hundred people could witness the same event and maybe no two individuals would see it exactly the same way. I just know I've had friends that would be here one day and gone the next, and all the embellished lies and bullshit starts flowing immediately. Rumors, innuendos, half-truths, outright lies. Even if I was there and saw it with my own squinting eyes, you can't argue. It's their truth. Or what they would like the truth to be, or how they interpret what they saw. *Rashomon*. Rewritten to include their moral twist to the story. And sometimes people may include themselves in the scene, even if they weren't present. When they weren't even born yet. Myth becomes history and history becomes myth. Then maybe they merge and it's hard to tell fact from fiction. What I'm laying down with this might not seem to be the truth to some, but it is the way I remember it. And I was the one who was there. History gets written by people who weren't there or who have preconceptions and agendas. They sometimes poison the well with misinformation, whether accidental or intentional. I want this to be a primary document. I lived it to write it.

One of the reasons for putting this all down after all the nightmares is to provide the truth. As unadulterated as possible. Though, as I've said, I pulled a few punches here and there. And I've changed a few names to protect identities, if not the innocent. For instance, "Hansons" is a made-up name. That crew was pretty far from being a lovable boy band. And the drug dealer referred to as "Bobby" is still alive, and I gave him the name in honor of Darby Crash's early moniker, Bobby Pyn. This guy even looks like a "Bobby" to me. If I wrote a screenplay about him, that's the name I would use. When I told him I was gonna put down my story and wanted to mention him, he was all for it and said it was okay if I used his real name. But I wanted to give him anonymity. Even though I left his world behind, I still like the guy. Of course, there were other name changes as well, but there's no need to reveal them.

Before continuing the story of my fortunes and misfortunes, I'm gonna pause a moment to take stock. So why did I decide to tell my story? Well, I was asked years ago and committed to the challenge. I'm glad I waited. There were a few times when it was almost too late. Really got through by the skin of my teeth.

A lot of fucked-up stuff has happened since then. I should have kept a running tally. But I'm not leaving any evidence. So I think now is a good time. Really, now? I guess it's as good of a time as any, right? And time is most definitely not on my side. I never wanted to follow the usual course of action. I figure I've done this and that, now I should sit here and write about it, that makes sense and is the natural course. I always thought I had it all worked out. Idiot.

I never wanted to blow through my wonder years like a normal, fucked-up, self-centered teenager and once I turned eighteen, then it's time to stop and start concentrating on my future. Who came up with that plan? School, job, wife, family, then retirement, then death. Like most everything, I did it backward. I thought I can enjoy my life and do whatever I want, and once I'm too old to do any more cocaine, then I can start working to put all this down.

What did I expect? I never was instilled with any kind of decent work ethic. My childhood was fucked. I had the responsibility of raising my siblings shoved on me when I was young. I had to bring up my younger brother and sister. Cook, wash, and raise those little rug rats and curtain crawlers. When I turned sixteen, it wasn't my problem anymore, so I ran. I hit the door and ran like a motherfucker, and I never stopped to look back. My sister and brother, for the sake of their privacy, and because everyone has their own side of the story, I'll leave out of this. I think they should tell their own Rashomon-like version. It all boils down to we were all there, and they just experienced a different sort of horror. I don't know how they...I don't know how WE all made it out alive and with our sanity still somewhat intact. But it's a small miracle that due to the abuse, psychological torture, and bad luck of the draw, they didn't turn out to be complete pieces of shit.

I've talked about all this before. I've had a few opportunities to document all this hell. I've even scribbled a few short pieces for a couple of rags, though I must admit those tales now seem dashed off. But things come in and out of fashion pretty fast, and my dirty, unmade bed has been taken to the curb. My old worn-out boots have been replaced with shiny high-heeled shoes. I can't polish this no matter how much spit shine I put on it. It is ugly, and nothing but. I'm sorry if those magazine editors got tired of slumming and heard their true calling.

More than a decade ago I read a memoir by a musician I've long admired. I had been looking forward to it for many months and had high expectations, but found myself disappointed. The reason? He always had to be the hero. Self-glorification. When anything went wrong, he was quick to pass the blame. Nothing was ever his fault. That's not the kind of book I have any interest in writing. The world has enough of those.

And I want to let this out once and for all, I'm busting at the seams. At times, my fingertips have been on fire pecking this out. To thine own self be true? My idea was to do everything you can do in this one life and to have no regrets. Know thyself, the unexamined life is not worth living, and all that jazz. But to push it as far as possible. Yes, I've had my share of pleasures and rewards. Sometimes I really thought that I couldn't or wouldn't ever write this stuff down. PTSD. Keeping my cards close to my chest. Still feeling the sting and MYO fuckin' B. Take whatever you want. If there's a Rosebud moment, something from my distant past that I might fixate on when on my deathbed, it's probably buried somewhere in here.

Confessional? That's definitely here. Some people confess just enough to make you think you're getting the full story. But what did they leave out? That's the first thing I want to know. I'd rather throw away the mask. And just because I'm admitting what I did doesn't mean I'm proud of leaving a trail of wreckage. There were many times I was a straight-up dick. Is it therapeutic? There are some things that I won't talk about, not because I'm ashamed, but personally I think they're so rotten that they still make me sick. It's nothing that I could get in trouble for, statute of limitations and all that. I just won't glorify it. But like they say, "Warts and all." I guess it's time to try to burn those bastards off. This is me, and these are my warts, this is my life, this is my art.

There's an old expression that goes, "Live fast, die young, and leave a beautiful corpse." Maybe I thought that was a cool idea when I was a teenager. But by the time I was twenty-five, I started to imagine showing up on a slab at the morgue, and for pathologists to look over my outsized body full of scars and tattoos and then wonder what kind of full or excessive life this fool must have lived. My body would be a road map of dangers and self-abuse. "Oh, my God, what do we have here? How did he get like this? Why did he do that? How did he survive this long? What finally did him in?"

I've woken up with tubes down my throat and a medic pumping on my chest. I know what that feels like. I've woken up in a hospital after an OD and turned to a visitor who had sat patiently by my side for hours, with the first words out of my mouth being, "Were you able to save the dope?" That was once my chief concern. It was all I had come to care about. In my lower depths, I figured things couldn't get any worse. (Oh, but they could!) Murphy and his fuckin' law.

If I were a painter, I would have painted the canvas black, shit on it, then burned it, then stomped it into the ground. Finally, an about-face and now I'm soaking it in bleach and water, trying to bring it back. As I said earlier, it's my story and I'm telling it so no one else can retell it. People rarely get a second chance. Especially when you've spent your life circling the drain. There might have been a time when I didn't want to think about not being here tomorrow. The ego will kill you every time. Now I'm happy I lived as long as I have and feel like I've done almost everything I've wanted to do. But to still be here, to see what waits for everyone tomorrow? No, thank you. I do get tired. If you've attended enough soirees, you know when to gracefully sneak out. Yeah, I feel sorry for the children who are inheriting this shell of a world. Dorian Gray, George Jetson, and eternal life might have sounded good one drunken evening. But smelling the burning bacon, hearing the distant trumpets, and seeing the writing, in dog shit, smeared on the wall, I've changed my mind.

If there is such a thing as reincarnation, I'll be the moth that dive bombs into the bug zapper. I'll be the squirrel that runs full speed into the headlights. I'll be the two-year-old child jumping into the gorilla's cage. You get the idea? I sometimes think it's too late to save this place, and I don't want to stick around for the last act. I don't want to sneak a peek into the back of the book. And I don't want to have to fight my neighbor for a cup of water.

If I was to leave one message, it would be that we know who did this, and if it's the last act that we do as a race of people, we should make the responsible parties pay. This might be part of my atonement? I feel I've said my apologies. I know I screwed up, but I've cleaned up my mess. I've made peace with myself. After going full speed, not looking back, and doing what I want, I'll take responsibility, and I do know when I'm wrong. Though being loaded out of my head didn't make the picture crystal clear.

I've been a junkie as far back as I can remember. I've been doing drugs and booze in one shape or another since I was nine. And during my teen years up into my twenties and thirties, there are periods where I draw a big blank. Times where I went non-stop, 24/7/365. Of course, it's going to escalate and as the party gets faster, your tolerance goes up, and you keep upping the dose. I upped it until I went as far as you could go. I flatlined more than once, and I never saw any light in that tunnel. Like I said, I'm not bragging, but I wouldn't be writing this if I didn't stop to at least catch my breath. Today I'm not loaded, and couldn't do this if I was, and if I didn't get "Hollywood sober." I'm not "straight edge" and I ain't no saint. I was in Las Vegas last month and I was drinking, pilling, and snorting. But as long as I don't have a needle full of dope shoved in my body somewhere, I'm "Hollywood sober," and that's a start.

Tomorrow? Like those alcoholics say, "One trip at a time." It's been years of abuse, so to wake up without a hangover and to take care of business is a whole new trip. Part of that trip means writing this story down. And that's what I'm doing. So I wanted to get that out of the way, and get this off of my chest before I jump into my side of things. Sometimes I do contradict myself, but I'll blame that on being a Gemini, even one who doesn't believe in astrology. I love this planet, but hate how people have shit all over it. I hate the few who rule over the many, and always have. But I love my dogs. I hate the status quo, and I rarely believe what you tell me. Somewhere in me, I still have hope for people. Then sometimes I feel like I don't believe in anything. But I believe in me. Or maybe I'm just bat shit crazy. That's one of the good things about not caring. All right, where do I start?

The friendships and camaraderie this music brought me means a lot. I put up many bands over the years. The number is well into the dozens. When I lived with Tammy, with Tom, with Mary, in punk rock crash houses, and by myself. How many bands, along with the occasional entourage they brought or hangers-on, had they picked up in town? Forty? Fifty? I'm not sure. A lot. Most of it was pretty low-key fun. Maybe we'd have drinks and take-out pizza and shoot the shit while taking turns being DJs. There are some salacious stories that I'll keep to myself. A few times people tried to crawl into bed with me. One time someone offered Tom and myself blow jobs if we'd share our dope. For the record, we were both embarrassed for the person and declined that desperate offer. But we gladly shared our dope. Another time, folks got rowdy and things got a little out of hand. I reached for my gun and told them in no uncertain terms that it was time to go. They were a little sore in the heat of the moment, but there were no long-term hard feelings. It's all water under the bridge. I won't name any names. I consider all of these people to be comrades and some were great friends. Unfortunately, more than a handful have passed away. But we shared good times.

It's the innocent moments with those guests that I most often remember. I will share one PG-13 experience. The band Raw Power from Italy stayed with us for a couple of days. Our equipment was set up in the basement, so Tom and I asked them if they'd play some songs for us. We went downstairs and they gave a command performance. It was great hearing songs like "You Are Fired" and "Fuck Authority" in that intimate and familiar setting. A very fond memory.

Now that I've gotten that out of my system, let's return to the story. History is written by the winners, right?

I've never won anything.

13

SINCE I WALKED OUT OF TOM'S apartment on the day he died, I've lived a half dozen more lifetimes. There are hundreds of new stories. Things go up and down. I'm not 100 percent sober, still to this day. When I'd go on tour, "not drinking" meant having a bottle of red wine and a bottle of white wine on the rider. I'd chug the red wine and the white wine was the chaser. On a few occasions, I puked it up in dressing rooms and parking lots. But when I got home I was motivated to quit drinking for a while. Now I drink on occasion, but I'm seldom out of control. And I quit doing "hard drugs." I haven't injected anything for years. I can't remember the last time, so it's gotta be close to ten years? I'm doing a *lot* better than I was twenty years ago, but I'm still far from being as healthy as I would like. I went in to see my doctor about doing something about my hep-C, and the medical team wanted to do a gastric bypass on me to be able to get to my liver because I was so fat. They thought it would have been almost impossible to probe around down there without nicking something and having me bleed out. It would have been very risky. I didn't want a gastric bypass because I've read up on it and I was scared of trading one problem for another.

I decided to get a combination of a modified sleeve/half bypass, so I'm still getting my protein and can try to continue to heal as best I know how. I lost some weight, then they went in to do a liver biopsy and said, "I don't know who told you that you had hepatitis, but your count is so low that it's not traceable." I don't know to this day if that doctor was completely fucking with my head just because she could (remember she didn't appreciate my sense of humor, which she interpreted as a smart-aleck remark), or if I really was sick at that time. By losing all this weight, my diabetes had started to go into remission. But not before I pushed that to the point where I had to have operations on both feet.

Here's how that happened. Poison Idea toured Europe and I never took care of myself. I was a wreck. I stepped on some glass and let it go. It kept getting worse. My foot became so infected with gangrene that I flew into Portland and drove straight to the hospital, where they started hacking off bones and toes. Three operations, two bone removals. That was a wake-up. I know that sounds cliché but sometimes these things snap ya out of it. So, I had the stomach surgery, got on a diet, and lost weight. Actually, they wanted me to lose weight *before* the surgery, to prove my determination and resolve. I did that in part by going to the pool regularly. Swimming was the perfect exercise for me. Coupled with watching what I ate, it had me losing almost fifty pounds. There are times I wonder if I even needed the surgery. But I got it. And here I am. Things change.

Let me tell a story that illustrates the difference between then and now. There was a time maybe twenty years ago when I got on a plane to Austin. Ostensibly, it was to see my brother who had moved down there. But there was a darker reason: I wanted to sample the drugs that were so powerful they were leading to people dropping like flies from overdoses. I can't remember specifics, but bags of dope often are labeled with some deadly sounding name. It could be "poison" or "death's door" or "grim reaper" or 'final exit," something like that, and I think might have been the case down in Austin. The media jumped on it. The deaths made the national news, and I was intrigued. Yes, that's pretty fucked, but I've explained that's the way it is with hardcore junkies. Just like when Steve died and Tom wondered aloud that the shit that did him in must have been high quality. This is how junkies think and it led me down to Texas to try my luck.

Another thing I wanted to do was to visit Six Flags. I figured it would be a fun experience so I bought day passes for me and my brother. I was anxious to check out the rollercoasters and some of the other rides. Then something unexpected happened which left me frustrated and embarrassed. I waited in a long line for one of the rides, only to be told when my turn finally came that I was "too obese." They would not let me on the ride. I was angry and humiliated and left the park immediately, not getting a penny's worth of value.

As for the drugs, they were disappointing. Absolutely nothing special. It turned out that the people who were dying were inexperienced people from the suburbs. The dope was not especially potent. It was just that the victims did not possess the tolerance of serious users and it did them in.

So, now I'm sober (at least by my standards), and I'm one hundred pounds lighter than I was before the surgery. I'm healthier than I was in my late twenties. In addition, my day-to-day outlook would change. On NW days when it was wet and all, well, my mood would often reflect that. But now that I'm sober, the weather doesn't get me down the way it sometimes could.

People tell me I look better. I guess we all change. I still get a new tattoo every now and again. I started getting them when I was a teenager, well before it got so fashionable and commonplace. It still seemed pretty underground when *RE/search* put out their "Modern Primitives" issue. If I was a rebellious kid now, I might look for some other way to express my individuality. For me, tattoos remind me of things. Sometimes they are souvenirs of places I have visited, like Japan or the Basque Country. I suppose they are kind of a road map of my life. Just wait until I am on the slab at the morgue and the coroner gets a look at me.

I was interviewed on a podcast recently and one subject of conversation centered around old punk rock records I had in my collection. This happens a lot, which is to be expected when you named an early recording *Record Collectors Are Pretentious Assholes*. I'm okay with nerding out about records because I love them so much. I just don't have many valuables left in my collection anymore. Some fetch top-dollar now, but I parted with those long ago, mostly for drug money. Another way I'd earn money was to sell things I'd find in the streets to a pawn shop. But when I was desperate, I'd hock other things. Like a cool piece of musical equipment I had bought for Mary's birthday. I took that to the pawnbroker, got my money for dope, and forgot about it. It didn't matter whether I'd gotten crack or heroin or something else—hell, it could have been anything from nasty prison-quality pot to high-grade Beverly Hills rock-star cocaine, a week or two later I'd remember and have to think about hustling up cash. There were times I would race downtown on the day my claim ticket would expire. I never lost anything important like Mary's present, but there were times I made it with minutes to spare. Just got in under the wire. And I paid a lot of interest in the process. Fortunately, those days are in the distant past. But, no, I don't have many collectible records. What would I do with them anyway? I suppose I could turn up the volume and play them loud after the post-nuclear apocalypse. Oh, right, we might not have any power. Well, I suppose I could use them to signal the cannibals in the hills. One thing I do have is an XXXL T-shirt covered with band buttons. I started it many years ago and it's almost fully covered. Occasionally I'll pick a few buttons off to accessorize my jacket or coat, but mostly it's like an ongoing work of art.

Years ago, in the early eighties, I went to a punk rock matinee show and part of my fashion attire for that day was a small dead dog hanging off the side of my leather jacket, wrapped in a plastic bag. Yeah, it was something an asshole would do. I now have two rescue dogs that I gladly dedicate a good chunk of my time to raising. When they're sick, I chew up food and feed them from my own mouth, and I take them on their daily walks and pick up their shit and wipe their little dog asses. When they're sick and have to sleep in their crates, I set up a bedroll on the floor and sleep next to them, with my hand in their cage. Things do change. The march of time. As I say all through this, the only constant in life besides death is change, and although it took me years to shake some bad habits, I'm not taking the worst ones to the grave with me.

I waited until I had forgotten everything I ever learned in school about math to go back to community college to try to get my GED. After a few months of blindly fumbling around, having no idea what I was doing, I got private tutoring lessons from Buns' widow and with a couple shots at the test, I passed. I waited almost four decades after I walked out of the school doors to go back and get the equivalent to my high school diploma. I guess it wasn't too late after all.

After I moved back in with Mary, we became a couple again (a couple of what?). I always loved her, and she's always stuck by me. She's still sober. She went to law school and passed the bar with me encouraging and championing every single day of her journey. I was able to vicariously experience the struggles and accomplishments along the way. I helped her study for her exams, I invested a lot of my time into helping her succeed and reach her goals. I sacrificed a lot. The traditional roles were reversed. I became a house husband who cooked the meals and kept house. Taking care of her daily needs became as important as the band. I created flash cards and helped her study. I did everything I could to create the best possible learning environment. The most important thing I did was when she had no drive, which was often the case, I was there to encourage her. I was a constant cheerleader. It was difficult at first, but she did great. She got her degree and passed the bar. I always knew she could do anything. I guess that's kinda the motto of this whole smoking pile of rubble; I really saw for myself it's never too late. You could have never have told me this when I was sixteen because I would have never believed it.

We'd still go out to concerts a few times a year. Many different genres. It could be anything from the twee-pop of Belle & Sebastian to an extreme metal band. For instance, there was a popular European black metal band that came through one time that Mary liked and I was able to get us backstage. Maybe someone told the band who I was or maybe they just recognized me. They were very nice, telling me how much they liked PI. The band started apologizing while putting on their corpse paint: "We're really punks, ya know." I told them, "It's cool, don't worry about it, we like your music."

I went to a show that was attended by the father of a big rock star. He was hard to miss. He strutted like a peacock and said his name for all to hear. He even wore a jacket or cape with his name spelled out, as if there could be any doubt. His son has been accused of sexually harassing young girls. Rumors are rampant, though it would be easy to name a dozen other musicians who have this kind of reputation. But looking at the father, you could kinda see where he gets it. He came up to the balcony, and I fantasized for a brief second what it would be like to push this blowhard over the edge. I wasn't the only person that had that idea. Another guy from the scene suggested it. I think he was half-kidding? But when the rock star dad left later that night, I shouted out to him, "Hey, _____, I hope you treat women better than your son does!" I think it caught him off guard and stunned him. For once, this loudmouth was speechless.

Another thing we did was make a trip to Montana. I wanted to see all the old places. I figured it might jog my memory and help kickstart this book. Like people often say, all those childhood places seemed much smaller. The buildings, the yards, the streets I walked and rode my bike, the old hangouts, even the surrounding nature. Memories did come flooding back, some the source of nightmares, plus a few good ones. I had wanted to stop at some scenic locales on the return trip, but I had run out of medication, so we had to hightail it back to Portland. Mary did the driving. The closest I got to seeing beautiful Montana nature was when I rolled down my passenger window and hurled puke out of a moving car.

After I first moved back in with Mary and started cutting back on the dope, I started focusing on Poison Idea more and more. This meant reviving the band. People sometimes wonder how the band could continue without Tom. The thing is the band existed before Tom (he came in around Mark III), it existed after he left us stranded in Europe, and it existed after he was back writing songs but no longer playing live. I'm the one constant in Poison Idea, and I can tell ya for certain that Tom would have approved of me carrying on the band without him.

At some point, I realized that we did have people who really dug the music and throughout the years it had all meant something to them. That's when I decided to lay down a rule. I don't care if you drink, I don't care if you do a line of speed, but anything that takes precedence over your playing, anything that you have to put before the music has to go. I'm sorry. I know that I spent years doing that in Poison Idea, but the music suffered for it, and I now wanted to make everything as good as we possibly could. I felt guilty for ripping people off and being substandard. It took a while. Band members came and went for a number of reasons, and a couple of people prioritized shooting up over playing music. I had done that long enough that I will never judge them. I fucking don't care what you do, but if you want to do this with me, this is the way it's gonna have to be. I want the band to be the best version of ourselves that we can be. That's all there is to it.

After a while, the band got really good again and wrote and played songs as well ever before. We'd learn new covers; I wanted to be a human jukebox. We traveled all over the place. I would occasionally still blow fire. One quick story about that. We played a show in New England once and the club owner called me into his office after the show. He was irate. He said, "I've only got two words for you: Great White." He was referencing the fire in Rhode Island a few years earlier that had killed one hundred. He then launched into some rant for a full minute. I remember thinking, "Hey, I thought you said it was only *two* words!"

The one thing that got difficult for me after I got sober was the emotion I would feel when I would sing certain songs. For instance, the song "Feel the Darkness" was about a friend of mine who was murdered. There are other songs that also bring back painful memories. It wasn't so hard to sing those songs when I was drunk or high, but sometimes when I was sober I'd be faced with reliving raw emotion. The only way I could manage while sober was to sing it on autopilot and not think too much about the words. Otherwise, my eyes would be leaking onstage.

We started putting out great records and playing tighter than ever. Eventually we did a studio album called *Confuse & Conquer*, plus more than a handful of singles and a live album.

We weren't a band that spent months in the studio. We knew perfection was unobtainable, but we tried our best, took a shot, then moved on to the next thing. That was our method. We liked to be well-rehearsed and then work fast, with focus.

We also played a lot of live shows. We went to Europe multiple times; we made cross-country tours; we played Mexico City. I liked visiting new places. And the touring made us a tight unit.

Most of the tours went well, with one or two exceptions. One of the European stints was especially rough. We played fine or even better than fine, but I had health issues and there were a string of complications. Along with that, there was a pretend manager (more like a "mismanager") who ripped us off for thousands. We played thirty-plus shows in Europe and came home broke. Death would have been too kind.

But we somehow managed. I bounced money around to get things done. I'd always pay the guys first and then sit on part of my share, the goal being to stockpile some money that I could put back into the band to keep us going. I took the money from one of our shows and bought a dozen shirts and had them silk-screened with the logo on it. At the next show we sold those. With that money, we bought more shirts and ordered some hats. PI continued to flip our merchandise and parlay what we had until we had enough to go into the recording studio. I don't know how it is for other bands, but we tend to make about half as much in merch sales as our guarantee from the club. If a club guarantee is 4K, we could probably expect to make about two grand in merch sales—though it's not pure profit, a lot of that will go toward covering expenses. Eventually, we took our savings and recorded new songs, which we had pressed onto vinyl. Then we put it out ourselves. Back on the same label that Tom and I started in the 1980s.

I'm still doing that, and I recently put out a compilation record with nothing but what I think are the best bands in Portland, though I have learned the hard way that compilations are seldom moneymakers. I'm really proud of that record and was happy when an excited journalist from the UK called to say how much he liked it, but I still haven't made back my investment. I really don't know what I'm doing. I just have a feeling if I stay busy and keep doing whatever pops up and sounds good, then I'll stay out of trouble.

Things would come to a screeching halt, though. We had a world tour planned for 2017, but a couple of the guys weren't getting along and then one of them quit, which left us high and dry at the last minute. I figured maybe it was time to cut our losses and shut the band down for good. So I thought, let's play one final hometown show and go out with a bang. I figured I had taken Poison Idea as far as we could go. We made some great records, played some great tours. I figured we atoned for all the years of shitty shows, so once that was done, I decided to pull the plug and put the old bastard down. We didn't crumble in the middle of a tour or fall apart onstage.

So, in late December of 2016, we played what at the time I was sure would be our last show. It was a special night at Liquor Store because so many of the old guys came back and played, including Chris Tense, Dean, a few guys from *Feel the Darkness* (Myrtle, Hippy, and Aldine), plus a couple of soldiers who joined up after the millennium (guitarists Jimmy and Jeff). We had guys onstage from every decade of the band's existence: eighties, nineties, two thousands, tens. I can honestly say that it felt great to play with each of them. Despite all the drama over the years, we were a loyal brotherhood. When the band started, it was a group of kids from fucked-up dysfunctional families who bonded over a love of music. Sure, there was some in-fighting along the way, but we were still connected, along with the bandmates that would follow.

We gave it a fitting funeral, a memorial and a proper wake. Now it's over: RIP. I wrecked a lot of stuff throughout my life, but with this one we just turned the keys. On, off.

14

RIGHT NOW, I'M UNEMPLOYED. LIKE a lot of people. But I actually do want to work and will take whatever I can get. I always thought, "Why work all your life until sixty-five and then retire when you can run around and then when you're ready to settle down, start working then?" Maybe this is the reason why? My band and our friends used to say, "Don't be unemployed, be unemployable." I think we stole that from some crust punk band. That's all fine and good if you have any kind of support to fall back on, some security. And also if you didn't spend the younger part of your life raising absolute complete hell wherever you went.

I've put the word out with friends and on social media that I'm looking for a job. In my lifetime, I've tended bar, cooked at restaurants, been a bike messenger, done construction and landscaping, been a garbageman, a DJ, worked in clubs and retail, all sorts of shit.

Fashion was always appealing and I regret not getting my foot in the door with a clothing store many years ago when I had the chance. I've always valued being around old people, for their life experience and wisdom, so I've thought about working in eldercare. Tending to their needs. It wouldn't be glamorous, but it might be a good fit for me. I used to think about going to bartending school, but working in a bar might be a tough place to stay substance-free. Not just because of the availability of booze at a discount, but because of cocaine and whatever else is floating around. Too many temptations.

Someone told me about this hippy restaurant right down the street from where I'm now living (let's call it "Greedy Planet"). They were looking for a delivery driver, they needed one immediately. This instant. I have a perfect driving record, I can now pass a drug test, and I know this city.

So, through the chain I went, one interview, then the next. It went well. Finally, I got to meet the owner for the final interview, the last hurdle. But as he walked in, I immediately saw the look of recognition on his face. Then the forced smile and the nervous sweaty handshake as he said he would call me. I knew right then I would never work there.

I'll take anything! One of the last jobs I had was mopping up come and throwing guys out of boner boxes in the adult arcade, fer chrissakes.

Then an old acquaintance turned up whom I hadn't spoken with in years. She knew of something that anyone could get, and again there was immediate need. Maybe I could even start right away that day if I got the job. I get up early, shave/shower, put on my positive face, and go to this place. They relocated hoarders and elderly people out of their crumbling houses, then fixed them up, before putting them back in after the renovation. I got an interview and the guy seemed nice enough. "Now, you understand what we're doing here, you'll be working in houses that are pretty filthy." Yes, I can do that, I told him. "These people are hoarders. There'll be human waste, dead animals, syringes. You'll have to wear a Haz-Mat suit, and it's very hot and uncomfortable." I said no problem. I was eager to get started. "Great, well, our supervisor is running late, she should…oh, here she is now." Smiles, then the eyes meet.

I see the smile vanish quickly. And then I start thinking, "Where do I know this person from?" She didn't give me time to figure it out. Again with the forced grin, with the nervousness underneath. All I can figure is the old bar fights, a bloody face, maybe screaming some insane shit from a stage very LOUDLY. There was no way I was going to get that job.

Once people have an opinion of who you are, that's what they almost always stick with. There are people close to me who do the same thing. And no matter how much I will use myself as an example of how a person can change, that mindset is buried deep inside them. If you have any small measure of fame, people look at your Wikipedia page and take everything as fact. And your reputation follows you around. "Would you like to go out tonight and see so and so's band?" "No way, that guy's a Nazi, no!" I'll say, "Not anymore. He's in a Celtic-influenced world music band, and he's married to a black woman." But they'll say he's a Nazi. He might have been an idiot asshole thirty years ago. I might have been an idiot asshole thirty years ago. No one is entirely innocent. No matter that I knew when to step up and say no, no matter that I've figured I've been paying for all the fucked-up things I've done all along. It doesn't matter. I'm not a felon, but that really doesn't mean shit. People get railroaded for the color of their skin or for economic reasons every day. It doesn't matter if you're guilty or not.

I have been in jail a few times. I never served any hard time like Mike Ness (wink-wink). I could never write a song about "The Yard" with a straight face, no matter how much artistic license I took. Johnny Cash was great, and he could put himself in any song and bring it to life, but I always wondered what Merle Haggard, who did serious time, thought about guys who spent a night or two in jail and then milked it for a prison ballad. Did he think people did that for street cred or to glorify themselves? I don't think I could have written "Folsom Prison Blues" unless I had lived it and knew it from the inside. I once heard Dolly Parton, who has written thousands of songs, say, "I can't be no different than who I am." I like that. Not all troublemakers are outlaws. There's a big difference between passing a night in the drunk tank at the county jail and spending years in San Quentin.

When I think about doing hard time, I think of a hellhole in some far corner of the world, maybe a Thai jail for drug mules or the Turkish jails that were depicted in *Midnight Express* (which might have been a gross exaggeration, anyway). I don't think of a cushy jail in Scandinavia that is nicer than most of the homes I've lived in. One of the most extreme stories I know of prison hardship comes from the writings of Donny The Punk, a guy who was gang-raped in prison by dozens of inmates. He wasn't grandstanding. He had lived through it.

I've been busted for stealing food from a store, being drunk on the street, fighting, and not going to court for stealing the food. I was thrown in once with my buddy for taking on five guys and putting a couple of them in the hospital. It wasn't fun for us, and the system made it as uncomfortable as possible. But being a twenty-eight-year-old, six foot one, 250-pound shitkicker, it could have been worse. Looking back now, I wouldn't want to have been the old guy in for failure of child support or the hippy caught with a bag of dope. I remember screaming through the jail cell down to my friend down the hall, "Henry, you better still be a skinhead when I get out or I'm gonna kick your ass!" We were shaven-headed idiots, but we weren't skinheads. We both got out the next day, we weren't facing any time. But we played the part, terrorizing the weaker people in lock-up. Always playing some kind of part.

The next time I was in for failure to appear, I played the part of someone who could be facing a month or two, and I was indeed worried. Labor Day Weekend. The craziest thing I saw during that stay was some mentally unstable gentleman cheeking his meds and then crushing up whatever they gave him before smoking it and flipping out. These pills were known as "Kick Kits" and were given to addicts, much like in the old days they might give a little bit of liquor to an alcoholic prisoner to get 'em over the hump. By saving them up and taking them all at once he got a massive rush. It was definitely better than television. The guy snapped, freaked out. It was like he had superhuman strength from PCP. They called in the riot squad. It took a lot to subdue him. The guards came in with shields and clubs and beat the guy half-dead. One female guard hit him so hard that she came to work the next day with her arm in a cast or sling, I'm not sure which. I was surprised that she came back. Maybe there was no workman's comp and she needed the money? I can say the guy who took the beating didn't feel much pain. But it was brutal. I got out a few days later and wrote a song about it called "Jailhouse Stomp."

Man, that was a long time ago. When they still admitted mental patients to some kind of care facility instead of just hurling them onto the street. Or making it impossible for them to get any help in the first place. Not long ago, I saw a guy standing in the middle of the street naked, throwing shit and stopping traffic. The cops arrived, took him to jail, then spent time writing up paperwork. He's processed, and they ask him, "Do you use drugs?" He answered, "Well, yeah? Of course I do dope." And then it's, "Well, then this really isn't a crime issue, it's more of a drug problem." They cut him loose with an order to appear in court. Soon thereafter he's back, standing on the street naked, covered in shit and stopping traffic. A repeat performance, a return engagement.

I remember when they closed the mental hospitals. Yeah, I remember the mental hospitals. I even have a fond memory or two, because I booked my band to play at one. I had seen a Target Video of The Cramps playing the Napa State Mental Hospital, and I thought, well, we do have the Oregon State hospital right down the road. I figured it couldn't hurt to ask. A closed mouth never gets fed. So I called them up and asked to speak with the person in charge of activities. I told them I was in a band, and we wanted to play for the patients. That's all it took. That's how the first band I was ever in (The Kinetics) and my current band (Smegma) both played at Dammasch State Mental Hospital.

What do I remember about the show? Mostly that it was fun. I remember most of the people there seemed blown away that this could happen. Some of the punk elders, like Fred Cole and Greg Sage, seemed impressed that a young kid like me had the drive to line up this show. I was an adrenaline junkie, full of beans. I must have been sixteen, and I was one of the younger kids in the scene at the time. It wasn't like LA, where there were hundreds of twelve- and thirteen-year-olds in the scene. That show was a blast, and people who attended talked about it for years.

Fred Cole passed away while I was writing this book. It was a sad day for the Portland music scene. I can't overstate his importance to the Portland arts community. It was a loss that went beyond music. His guitar store had been a meeting place for us young punk kids. That's how I first got to know him. Later, I was lucky enough to share a stage with him, which was an honor. Dead Moon was a beloved band, obviously, but I was fortunate to be able to see all of his projects from 1978 on. Some are pretty forgotten. Zap Spangler, anyone? Fred was a good man and an anchor in the local music scene. Like Tom, I thought he would be around forever. A loss like that can slap you out of your complacency, at least temporarily.

We also recently lost Thor Lindsay, who was a big contributor to our scene, first with Singles Going Steady, then TK Records and other ventures. A tastemaker. TK had made a lot of money back when record companies had lots of money to throw around, in the days right before the bottom fell out of the record industry. Thor bought a nice house and a Cadillac. I always thought his mistake was that he didn't put more back into the company. (Come to think of it, doesn't "Thor's Mistake" sound like a decent name for a doom metal band?) Eventually, Thor sold off his stock to Capitol Records. I thought he could have built it up if he'd invested wisely. But when I think of Thor, I immediately think of how much he believed in Gift. He was our biggest champion. On multiple occasions, he told people he thought we had the potential to be the most popular nineties band to come out of Portland. I remember him lifting up our Gift CD and telling a large group gathered as he was closing up shop, "I would have bet the farm on Gift. I really believed they could have been our biggest local band." He thought we "coulda' been contenders."

Losing Tom, Fred, and Thor was hard for locals. The world is definitely a more boring place without those three. It's a crazy thing to me that time makes people age, grow, learn, forget, die. I want to take chances and risk failure to challenge myself and seize the day. Let's finish this story that we create ourselves. Stranger than fiction, stranger than truth.

In looking back over my life, it's probably normal to wonder about what I might have done differently. There were roads not taken that might have led to interesting places and situations. But, really, I think I would have done just a few things differently, which is how I suspect it would be for almost everybody. For instance, from a practical standpoint, I could have done selective service when I was a teenager. That way, it would look good on my record, I'd be getting an Army pension, and it would have been a short enough commitment that I wouldn't have missed much. And later,

I may have been able to get a government job, instead of being told "you'll never work here" at the post office because of the stain on my record. If I'd done a short hitch, I would have been young enough after getting out that I still could have done everything I wanted to with music, instead of just pissing my pants like I did in those late teenage years. I still could have fronted a punk band by the time I was twenty-two, with military service under my belt, and with benefits to show for it.

I also used to think about a career in the movies. I know people who moved away and got rich, including people who went to Hollywood and made millions. I had once thought about moving to LA so I could try my hand at acting. I would pay attention when I watched classic movies, not just to great actors like De Niro but also the character actors many don't notice. I used to watch a bunch of old classic black-and-white films and would often notice a character actor who was only on-screen for a few minutes. A small scene or cameo could make a big impression. For example, I saw an old movie called *Detective Story* on TV when I was a teenager. It wasn't the leading man Kirk Douglas I remembered (in fact, I thought it was Robert Mitchum), but a little-known character actor named Joseph Wiseman playing the part of a criminal that stayed with me. I wondered if I could have gotten a role as an alternative leading man or, more likely, a character actor. That would be more realistic. That was something I thought about doing and I wonder how it would have turned out. But when I think of those wealthy Hollywood types, I do wonder just how good that day-to-day life really is. I mean, a prison is still a prison even if it's made of gold. A jail cell made of gold bars is still a cage. And when you start doing everything for money, it's like you start wearing gold handcuffs.

There was a scene in *The Sopranos* where a depressed Tony is lamenting guys who get in touch with their feelings and become

15

WELL, I'M ALMOST FINISHED WRITING this. And, yeah, I'm still here. That was the plan all along. Luckily, for once the plan worked for me. The person who originally lit the fire under my ass to write this book in the first place, Adam Parfrey, passed away last year. Adam deserves a book of his own, and one day soon he may get one. But this is my small shoutout to him. Adam was a man of many masks. He was a prankster, a musician, a book publisher. He started with Amok Books and then ran Feral House Books. The story of how he wound up doing that, while not as violent and dysfunctional as my own path, was still every bit as interesting.

I really liked Adam. We met decades ago through the Portland writer Rene Denfeld. Adam and his wife had moved up here from LA, and he was looking into making some kind of music. I was already familiar with Adam's book *Apocalypse Culture*. It became something of a cult classic that made its way through my Portland circle. And I knew *EXIT* magazine, which he was involved with in some capacity, though I'm not sure of the chronology. But Adam's book was a hot ticket among my friends and Rene hooked him up with all my people. Treading cautiously at first, he was reluctant to allow me into his house. But it wasn't long before he became a friend to the whole band. I know that he thought it was kind of funny that Tom was a coke dealer, that I carried a pistol, and that almost everyone in the band used heroin on a daily basis. At least we didn't seem boring. But it didn't take long before Adam was puffing on the tin foil right along with us. I know for a fact that Adam was not into drugs before he got to Portland. I saw it all happen, and I watched as it picked up speed. If you hang out in a whorehouse long enough, you're gonna catch crabs.

I'm not exactly sure why Adam chose Portland. It was cheap back then and that might have been a factor. Portland had its share of interesting artists and writers in those days. For instance, Katherine Dunn, who wrote the cult novel *Geek Love,* was a pretty beloved figure, and she wrote columns for the local free weekly paper, the *Willamette Week*. Some of the writers intersected with the music scene. I got to know Richard Meltzer, a transplant from LA who moved up to Portland in the mid-nineties. He was a real character who had been a prolific author. He wrote novels, stories, criticism, poems, and songs (including a big hit for Blue Öyster Cult). If you know the song "Burnin' For You," then you know some of his words. Younger bands like The Minutemen wanted to collaborate with him. Meltzer had been in a punk band in LA called Vom and had hosted his own punk radio show called *Hepcats From Hell* on KPFK circa 1980. Darby Crash had appeared on that show right before he died. When I'd see Meltzer around, I'd playfully chide him: "Hey Meltzer, you killed Darby!"

By the way, it's a bit of an aside, but I remember exactly how I learned of Darby's death. I was in a punk club in Portland a week or two after Darby's suicide, and a guy from The Ziplocs who had just been down in LA reported the news to a few of us. He'd been at a show in LA and heard Black Randy reference it. How did I react when I heard the news? "So?" That's what I said. My favorite lyricist had died and that's how I reacted. "So?" As a seventeen-year-old punk in Portland, that was the attitude I wanted to project—cold, uncaring, and that life is fleeting and without meaning. You had to be hard. It was kind of fitting that Adam Parfrey and Feral House would publish a book on Darby called *Lexicon Devil*, and that it was subtitled *The Fast Times and Short Life of Darby Crash and The Germs*. Fast times and a short life is what I expected for myself when I was a teenager, including on that December night in 1980 when I casually said, "So?"

Poison Idea eventually did a couple of musical projects with Adam, but I always had the idea he was more into collecting people. He seemed to know everybody. His father was an actor in Hollywood, whose work I was familiar with. Anyone who knows a lot about Clint Eastwood movies knows Woody Parfrey. He was a pretty in-demand character actor. He's probably most famous for being in *Planet of the Apes*. I forget how it came up, but during one of the first times we talked, I mentioned something about the play *The Flies* by Jean-Paul Sartre. We spoke about all kinds of things, but he was blown away that this thuggish junkie not only knew of this play but could quote a few lines from it. Adam told me he was in a stage production of the play when he was in high school. He also had done Shakespeare in his teenage years. He even showed me a picture of him with one of his costars from a high school production: Heather Thomas, who went on to a big TV career a decade later and became a pin-up on bedroom walls. That pairing that would likely have shocked fans of either person, and Adam loved that. He was drawn to strange, unexpected, hard-to-imagine intersections.

Adam was impressed enough with my lifestyle and variety of interests that I was added to his collection of people. Aside from surrounding himself with strange characters from whom he would squeeze out whatever they had to give, Adam really did hang out with a lot of weirdos. I'm not saying everyone got used, but he had a lot of friends. (By the way, Adam would often end his letters with a phrase like *"beast* wishes" or *"*your *fiend.")* You'd go to his house and there would be a cat burglar, a cop, a dominatrix, a film director, a street thug, a magician, an architect, an epidemiologist, a drug dealer, a contortionist. Adam seemed to have one of everything. He was friends with conspiracy theorists and famous skeptics who debunked them. I know he hosted salons when he moved back to LA. I imagine they were pretty lively.

Adam had gone to high school in Santa Monica but moved up to Northern California for college and then bounced around. He worked at the famous bookstore The Strand in NYC and spent a fair amount of time in San Francisco. He once told me a story about finding rare signed first editions by writers like Zane Grey and Henry Miller in dumpsters and selling them for big bucks at City Lights. He was lucky that way.

One of my earliest memories of him comes from when he and his wife threw a party for Richard Meltzer, Kathy Acker, and a bunch of people I had nothing in common with except we were all in Adam's house. I don't remember many details, though I went with Mary and we spent time keeping to ourselves, drinking and playing pinball until we finally decided to slip out the basement door. That day, some of Adam's friends were nice and some were snobby. Here, I'm talking mostly about the artistic folks. But some of his connections were pretty questionable. I know because I hung out with scumbags and Adam was humored by these people. He found my scumbag friends interesting. Then Adam joined our club and we all started to get loaded. And, of course, everything that goes with the scoring of the drugs is a big part of doing it. A ritual almost: trying to connect, waiting, going to the meeting point, waiting some more. He almost seemed to be taking notes on this for a future book. Then we would get high and bullshit.

Adam enjoyed many of the stories I have since written down in this book and thought they should be published. He drew up a deal, gave me some money, and told me to write down all the stuff I remembered. But first we had to continue to get high.

And we got high the whole time Adam lived in Portland. We got high through major life events: his divorce (I'm not saying drugs had anything to do with that but it's easy to assume that they did), selling his house, moving into a loft, making more music. Throughout it all, we would get high.

One night, he sent me out to North Portland, to a part of town that was regarded as being sketchy and dangerous. It was also one of the few places I could go at 1:00 a.m. and score some dope. Adam gave me his platinum bank card, with his pin number clipped to it. He told me to withdraw an agreed-upon amount, go get the stuff, and come straight back. I went to the ATM (of course, I waited until I was in the ghetto to hit the bank), took out the cash, and stuck the card in the back pocket of my ripped-out jeans. Naturally, it slid directly out onto the ground. I went and got the stuff and drove his car back to the condo. Walking up to the front door, I reached into my back pocket and felt the breeze from the hole. The card with his pin number was gone. That was a hard one explaining to him. I could tell immediately that he didn't believe me. But as we were standing there, the bank called saying someone was trying to use his card to buy a couple of state-of-the-art TVs, and would he authorize it. He figured I did, in fact, fuck up, and he dismissed me without sharing the drugs. But at least he knew I did not try to fuck him over.

Another night, while high, Adam swerved into the oncoming lane while crossing the Ross Island Bridge. He hit another car head on. Everyone survived, but Adam was thrown through the window and skidded about fifty yards down the pavement. The next day, when I saw him in the Intensive Care Unit, he looked really bad. His parents were there by his side. But Adam kept trying to talk to me, asking if I would bring him some dope in the hospital. There was no way I was gonna do that. Even though I knew firsthand how fucked withdrawal symptoms are, I couldn't do it.

His family got power of attorney over him. The guy who made a record called "The Tards," a parody of mentally challenged people, was now borderline retarded. I don't know if it was spite, his family dividing up his assets and his business, or if it was just his will to live and his ego kicking in, but that fucker pulled himself up, dusted himself off, got back in the saddle, and got back into the game. It was really incredible.

After he recovered, he moved away but we kept in touch. Adam was a pretty loyal friend. When I went to live with my sister in Santa Barbara so I could kick drugs, he came to visit me. It meant a lot that he took time off from his business to drive up and spend a day with me. He lifted my spirits. And I remember one time he went to bat for Poison Idea. I guess there was an interview once with Carrie Brownstein of Sleater-Kinney, where she was asked about us by name and she said something dismissive. Something like, "That was the old, dirty Portland; we're the new, good Portland." This really bothered Adam on multiple levels. He called her a clueless trust-fund brat living in a gentrified world. I don't remember his exact words, but they were surprisingly blistering. I guess her comments had rubbed him the wrong way.

Adam always had a soft spot for Portland and tried to get back when he could. He missed friends and places. He always chuckled when he'd think of the neighborhood known as "Felony Flats." The name got him every time. Both LA and Portland have skid rows downtown, but the distinctive name of a white trash neighborhood in SE Portland really made him laugh. Adam came to town a few times when he had a writer doing a book event, most likely at Powell's Books or Counter Media. And he returned for Tom's funeral. I do know he was a little disappointed that day, because he thought a lot of the old crew had not really grown as people. He thought they were stagnating.

We became better friends than we ever had been, and I know he was very surprised when I stopped doing drugs, because he told me so many times. Then, about a year ago there was a misunderstanding about a post on social media. And in a rare moment of losing it, he just snapped. He posted something on my Facebook page and people jumped on it, clowning the evil king. He didn't like it. I tried to explain the situation a few times but I couldn't get through to him. As a result, he told me he wasn't going to put this book out, and he ripped up the contract. "Find yourself another publisher."

Then, about a month later, he had a stroke and fell down the stairs or fell down the stairs and had a stroke. I'm not sure which happened first. But he passed away. Just like that. I've had a couple of bad falls myself. When I was at my heaviest, it was icy out and I slipped on the landing in front of my house. I flew backward past the steps, striking my head on the concrete path. In that split second, I thought, "Oh, shit, this is it—of all things, a front porch tumble will be my end. Fuck!" Another time, I was bringing down boxes for mail order and fell off a high ladder, straight onto my back. Before landing I thought, "Oh, no, now I'm gonna be paralyzed." In both cases, I bounced right back up. Very sore, but without serious injury. You hear stories of people falling out of airplanes and surviving. I love stories like that. Maybe a rip cord doesn't release but a skydiver survives. On the other hand, there are stories of combat veterans surviving a war only to slip in the bathtub at home and die from a cracked skull.

He told a mutual friend of ours right before he died that he was upset we had a falling out. I'm sure I would have gotten around to extending the olive branch. I will always say I'm sorry, this whole fucking book is me saying I'm sorry, and I would have said it to him in a second. I think he would have liked this book. After he died, I decided to make it richer, and began adding many more stories to the last working manuscript he had seen. This is what he had urged me to do. I'm sure we could have worked out our differences given time, but whaddaya gonna do now?

16

PEOPLE SAY THAT THERE ARE two times in a man's life when he cries: when his mother dies and when his dog dies. I don't know if that's true, but my first dog, my best friend and loyal companion, passed right around the same time as Adam. I still miss him every day. He had some kind of cancer and we took him to the vet. Five thousand dollars later, they said he was cancer-free. I knew he was weak from the ordeal, so I would take him out in a stroller every day, trying to get him healthy and able to eat again. I know the fresh air and our companionship were good for him. For more than a decade, we had been going to parks and dog runs. We liked making long walks through the side streets of our neighborhood. Sometimes I'd spot fruit trees and bushes along the way and the next time I'd bring a small bag and pick fresh apples, pears, and blackberries. There were a lot of crows in my part of town and once I saw a few of them team up to dive-bomb a hawk and chase it off. I've always liked observing nature. Going for walks with my dog could be the highlight of my day. And now it was sad to see him struggling.

When the total eclipse of the sun happened, I took a handful of mushrooms and we stood outside together. He was really weak but he stuck his head hard against my neck, almost like saying, "It's all right." I'm sure it was a combination of me being high as hell and wanting him to be okay and not be afraid. Part of me was starting to wonder if we were keeping him alive because he meant so much to us, despite how much he was obviously suffering. That we were selfishly putting our wishes ahead of what was best for him. Maybe he was ready to go, but we weren't ready to let go. It would have been more humane to put him down, to end his pain, but I just didn't want to think of a world without him in it. I've told this to other pet owners and it resonated. They had the same nagging guilt. Our dog still wouldn't eat so we wound up taking him back to the vet again. They said he had been overtaken by cancer and that we should euthanize the next day. We went home and he died that night. He truly was "man's best friend," with a love and loyalty I can only hope to receive in the future.

When my dog died, I was knocked for six. It took something out of me. I had a high threshold for pain, but in terms of sadness this was a benchmark, right up there with losing close friends. I was so distraught I needed to get away for a few days. I went to NYC for a change of pace and some distractions. I kinda just wanted to "take the air" and tool around the town and be alone with my thoughts. I wanted to walk across a bridge. See the water. Maybe take the train out to Coney Island. Maybe see the place Tony Soprano dreamed about, though maybe that was Asbury Park. I didn't want to go to culinary hotspots or anything like that; I prefer comfortable neighborhood favorites anyway. Just taking the subway here and there and walking around was entertainment enough. Without trying, I stumbled upon the Flatiron Building, saw protesters outside Trump Tower, wound up outside the Broadway Theater where Bruce Springsteen was having his one-man show, watched as scam artists on the street tried to fleece tourists, and many other things.

I did meet up with a few friends and that was good for me. For instance, I got together for lunch with Diane Kamikaze, the great punk DJ from WFMU. She's come to see PI a few times over the years and I've enjoyed being on her show. She's very knowledgeable, and now that I have my own show, we have even more to talk about. We met for lunch one day near the apartment I was staying in at Stuyvesant Town. We talked about this book and she stressed how important it was for me to finish it and document what the punk scene was like from the inside. A primary document. She thought it was important for music books to be written by people who were actually there. There were too many coming out that weren't. On my last night in town, I went out to Astoria and had dinner with a family at their favorite local Greek restaurant. This was the couple I stayed with in Little Italy when we played CBGB. They had since moved to Queens after becoming parents of twin daughters. The next day I made my way by public transportation to the airport. Being able to get around on the subway by myself was something I had wanted to master and that was a good test, since it involved making a couple of transfers. Back home, I had a NYC subway map on my wall, right next to a *NY Post* cover of Amy Winehouse's death ("No No No") and flyer of a James Brown concert in Manhattan that the "Godfather of Soul" did not live to see. I'd look closely at that map every now and again and I had a general understanding of the subway system. It felt good to be able to navigate my way around the city. When I got home, I was still very sad about my dog dying, but the trip helped me clear my head for a few days.

Then my father died. Without warning. It seemed like everything was falling apart and the planets were going crazy. As far as loyalty and love? He had his life, I had mine. That cord was cut. My father was out of my life before I was of legal age. I only met with him a few times in adulthood. Once a recovery program insisted I contact family and reestablish communication. I told them they were demanding the impossible. I had no idea where my old man was. But they were persistent, and giving up was not an option. "You gotta do this." Eventually, I found him. Another time, my sister drove me to see him in Eugene, where he was running a bar. It was a total surprise. My sister had loaned me fifty bucks and the way she wanted me to pay her back was to go and see my father. She asked me to give her a few hours of my time on the weekend. I actually thought we were going to a movie, or that she wanted me to help her move furniture. When I got in the car, I had no idea where we were headed. We spent a couple of hours making small talk in the bar and then headed back. The last time I saw my father was when I was living that hellish existence on Foster Road more than twenty years ago. He looked me up for some reason that's now long forgotten. I never saw him again after that, though we would speak on the phone occasionally. A short conversation every year or two.

People ask if my parents ever saw me play. My dad didn't. I don't know what he would have made of it. He had played in a surf combo when I was small. He was a pretty good player; he had chops. When I was growing up, he always had a guitar or two lying around, including a really nice Gibson. My mom actually did trudge out to see me once at the beginning, when I was playing in Smegma. For her, it was probably a noisy, tuneless mess, but she found a few positive words of encouragement. She proudly thought, "That's my boy!" when she saw me onstage. My dad couldn't be bothered. Though when he was on his deathbed, he did say he was proud of me.

A lot of people who were important in my life are gone and I'm still here. That was the plan. To finish this book. And looking back, you see that the more things change, the more they stay the same. I'm older, but I don't feel older. I feel sore. Sometimes I'm tired, sometimes really beat, but I do think about tomorrow.

The future, the kids. I live in a neighborhood with a college down the street and I see the young people. The guys who look like extras from that old movie *Newsies*—a waxed handlebar moustache, suspenders, and spats. Girls with bald heads and facial tattoos. All thinking they're the first ones to sport this look. We always think that. When I was seventeen years old and wore warpaint, a mohawk, and carried a samurai sword, I thought I was the first one to do this. I wasn't. Oswald Spengler wrote about the kids of Roman senators who would dress like the Northern Germanic tribes that eventually sacked their civilization. The Vandals, the Goths. Rich kids wearing fur, animal bones, and fronting like warlords. Is it that different than kids in rural Nebraska identifying with Crips and glamorizing and romanticizing violence? What do I think of the kids now? When I was young and living with Glenn's mother, I would listen to her stories about living through World War II and watching the world change. I was fascinated by it. Growing up as a kid in the punk scene, and practically being raised and educated by older punks and artists, I respected them and everything they knew. I've never been an ageist, I just never got a lot out of people younger than me, but with time I've learned to see more in them.

Some cultures revere their old, ours are disposable. But then again, snobs come in all forms and ages. And when I had one of my surgeries, and was almost forced to get on the internet, I befriended a lot of kids on social media. The kids were all right. Some of 'em.

Everyone has their own story. Some kids would tell me their problems or even ask me for advice. I can't see into the future, but I did my best. At times, I almost felt like a parent. A young guy from the East Coast confided in me that he was thinking about suicide. He was strung out on dope, he never had a family, it sounded familiar. I would talk with this guy and just speak openly and honestly. If I could do it over, would I? Probably for the most part, but I wouldn't have done this particular thing or that particular thing. He listened. He got his shit together and went back to school, graduated, and got a good-paying union job. He's now married with a family. I know it wasn't me that changed his life, but standing outside and looking in kinda made me proud. I've met a lot of kids and befriended them, and it's made me feel good, being able to call them my friends. I really love some of these people.

My brother and sister both have happy, healthy families, with smart, wonderful children. There's a lot of good kids out there. I'm sure there are plenty of worthless, spoiled brats out there too, but maybe the kids of the early twenty-first century give us rays of hope. Kids today are facing different challenges. In school, they practice lockdown drills the way my generation practiced fire drills. There have been so many school shootings in recent years. It's a different world. The one thing I'll say about that is that I don't blame art for mass shootings. I don't blame *The Basketball Diaries*— the book by Jim Carroll or the movie with Leonardo DiCaprio—for Columbine. Tim Yohannon once said to me, "Evil always wins." I laughed about it at the time, but sometimes when I look at problems today and some of the leaders in charge, I wonder if he might have been right. But maybe the young generation and the kids of the future will learn not to make the same mistakes.

The world is full of happiness, tragedy, and everything in between. One of the things that drives me nuts about social media is that every once in a while, I'll see a parent post something on their child's page saying something happened and they are no longer with us. They're saying goodbye and thanking everyone for being there. I'll then go back and look at our FB friend timeline and read over the conversations we had and then that makes me want to shut it down. I got on this thing to have a good time, not become infected with depression. It's a virus. The bullying.

All the fake information. Technology, the ultimate lie. And the eagerness to condemn someone and get in on that warm, mob-rule feeling.

We live in polarized times. People on the far left call people who don't agree with them "fascists" and "racists," while people on the right label people who don't agree with them "communists" and "libtards." That shuts down all dialogue. The world isn't all black and white. There is a lot of gray. Sometimes people have their bubbles burst by politics and become outraged. That's nothing new to me. I've always been pissed off by injustice. I say, "Welcome to the club." When Poison Idea stopped playing about two years ago, we did one last show. It was after the presidential election, and a few weeks before the inauguration. I said something to the crowd about, "Okay, we fucked that up, now let's all work together and try and fix it." All of us, working together. Let's not let the hysteria of the internet divide us. At first, before they seemed to fall in line with the party, some Republicans were actually calling the president on his shit. My point was that not all Republicans are evil, and people have to work across party lines and divisions. Pay more attention to what politicians do, not what they say. The next day someone wrote that I said something supporting Trump, and that is not at all what I said. They take a phrase out of context and spin it. And that snowballed into someone saying, "Wow, I always had respect for Jerry, I guess fuck him now." Just like that. Take it easy, people. We're lucky enough to have choices in this life, and I use mine every day. Someone asked me recently what makes me happy. Well, it changes with my mood from day to day. Some days I just like being left alone, other times I like company. But one thing that I always want is to be understood. I hate being misunderstood.

17

Now I STAY BUSY, BUT IT'S easy to get caught up in the instant gratification/short attention span of the next internet search. I discovered pretty quickly that I can disappear down that rabbit hole for hours at a time. Then there's social media. And sometimes more "games." I do try to correspond and keep in touch with friends, though I'm not always the most prompt and there aren't many lightning fast turnarounds. A local guy told me I should "friend" a woman from the old LA punk scene. I said, "Dude, I talked to this person before, she's the only person I've ever encountered who slurs her writing." But he convinced me so I reached out. What did I get? Blowback. She accusingly wrote back, saying, "You Are Not Richie Dagger!" This is a reference to a Germs song that I used to name my publishing company. I guess she didn't think I was worthy. My verdict: listen to your gut, always go with your first impression, never hesitate, and don't listen to imbeciles. Lesson learned. Then there's all the finger-pointing when politicizing issues. Just recently I stumbled on a comment page where a few people were debating the dark, underlying, politically incorrect agenda of a superhero movie (*Joker*). What? Geez, people. It's lightweight throwaway entertainment! Who takes this stuff seriously? Whatever makes their toes stand up in their Vans. It's just sad. Aren't there enough real fucking problems in the world without these swarming gnats?

Speaking of Hollywood, I did have an odd experience not too long ago. I was in an airport flying home from a tour. I got stuck in one of those long, winding lines that you go through as you make your way to the security checkpoint. You know, the ones where you see people behind you and that you start walking away from them but then you wrap back around and there they are again. I don't remember exactly what I was wearing, but it was probably a lot of rings, maybe a studded bracelet, a band T-shirt, a long rocker coat, and I was probably either carrying musical equipment to take on to the plane or I had a bag plastered with various band buttons and stickers. Not to mention the visible tattoos. I kept seeing this one dude staring at me. I wondered if I knew him or if he mistook me for someone else. But after passing this guy a few times, it dawned on me that he was a famous actor. I just couldn't put a name to a face. I kept looking back at him and he'd be looking right at me, smiling. I figured I'd remember once I boarded my plane but I didn't. It kept bugging me, so the next day I called a film buff and described him. Within minutes, I was sent back a picture that was a perfect match. It turned out to be Bradley Cooper, who was in pre-production of *A Star Is Born*. I figured that he had no idea who I was, but could easily guess that I was a professional musician, and he was looking everywhere, taking mental notes, to help build his character. Either that, or he just wondered, "Who is this fool?"

I should say that our band isn't one that has a lot of celebrity fans. I suppose we were more of a "people's band." I never got excited about celebrities coming to our shows, not that we had many. Though you may remember that I was excited when the wife of one of the guys from the MC5 came to see us. I guess she wasn't a celebrity, but that's how much that band had meant to me.

After we disbanded, I threw myself into other projects. Such as the writing of this book, my radio show, and the running of my

every week. There are no rules, and I'm having fun making it up as I go along. My interaction with the public is the most fun and rewarding part of the gig. It can be pretty comical. Even when I'm mumbling at 'em, there is a rapport. I have a feeling I won't be doing the show much longer. There is too much other stuff demanding my attention. But, right now, I look forward to these early Friday mornings.

I still actively seek out new music. It could be the latest flavor from England, or a forgotten classic of Americana, like, say, Dock Boggs. Or maybe a local band catches my ear and I go see them live. Maybe I'll want to put out their next record on my label. There is so much stuff available, both audio and visual. And more coming every day. For instance, I really thought I had seen every picture taken of the Pistols, but new books are still coming out. I just saw one with a bunch of photos I had never seen. I used to have a poster of the Sex Pistols album cover on a room upstairs in our house. Mary would make fun of me for it. She'd say the band only made one album, that their legacy is fewer than forty minutes, how can you still care so much after all these years? As for sounds, both new and old, there is so much hard-to-find audio available with just a few clicks of the keyboard. In some ways, it's a great time to be alive. Music means as much to me as it ever did and it will until the day I die.

18

I STARTED THIS BOOK IN earnest about four years ago. My first draft was lost when my computer died. Backup, you say? I didn't need no stinking backup! What an idiot I was. Man, did that piss off Adam. When I related the news, he pretty much gave up on me right then and there. It was like I had lost his ATM card all over again. You could hear the disappointment and exasperation in his voice. But it was a challenge, so I worked twice as fast and wrote it all down again and submitted it. Okay, I might have rushed it a bit and taken some shortcuts in my haste. I might not have bothered retelling some stories, and I might have quickly brushed over others. Adam wanted me to spend more time revising, but at least I had delivered on a promise.

Then came the misunderstanding and the falling out. It took me a month after Adam died to decide to pick it back up. I was determined to get rid of the typos and grammatical errors that had bugged him, and add scores of more varied stories he wanted me to tell. He wanted more detail, so I decided to unpack some of the anecdotes that I had mentioned but hadn't really sketched out, and put in more thoughts and observations, which he had greatly encouraged. I wanted to make it ten times better than it had been, and I was determined it wouldn't be a hack job. I committed then to putting in the time and doing whatever it takes to see this project through. I figured nobody else is gonna do this, so I better jump on it. I decided to reach out to an old friend who knows my stories well and who had been encouraging me from the get-go. He and Adam had been friends, and Adam used to urge him to help me years before I actually had the patience to pull up a chair and start putting my story down. Would he be willing to help me improve and expand a manuscript that was beginning to gather dust? Could he start immediately, as in pronto, Tonto?! The answer came quickly: he was all in.

While I've been writing this book, one punk memoir after another has been hitting the shelves. For the most part I've avoided them because I didn't want to be distracted or influenced. Maybe I'm too close to it. Occasionally I'd pick up one of the autobiographies that I thought had real potential, only to be disappointed. Some came across as total fluff. A lot of name-dropping, but no waves-a-making. This happened a few times, usually when I was trying to kill time at a bandmate's house or if a book had been left lying around at a venue. Or, like I said at the outset, maybe the subject always felt the need to come across as the hero. A young musician was telling me about three punk memoirs he had just read where each author claimed to have "invented" hardcore. They join dozens of others. I was thinking about one guy the young musician was telling me about, and I thought, "Wow, so much for surprises. Anyone within earshot of him has heard his stories a couple of times over. Like an old man slowly sinking into a bath." Nah, that's not fair, he had an interesting life, inventing hardcore. Before he disowned it. But now that he has waited long enough, that's all good. And the kids are all right. As long as they stay off his lawn. So, yeah, I know, I missed the first, second, and third waves of hardcore inventors writing books about how they blazed a trail and started it all. *C'est la vie*, and blow me down. Who's the new token Bukowski of the old and deaf?

My writing, like love, comes in spurts. When I started writing this book, I could only write a page or two and then I'd get a bad headache and have to take a long break. Or I'd have to take a drink. Not from putting in long hours, but from trying to remember the details. And that sucks. I hated it. I found myself shaking. Don't tell anyone, but I'm supposed to be carefree. Bravery has nothing to do with it. Not caring, that's how you can kill things. Brain cells. I had once thought writing this book would be a piece of cake. You know, sort of like "Caveman write when want."

But it's been hard work. There were times I just scribbled something that made no sense. Sounding like someone standing on the street, screaming. At times, it was like I was exorcising demons. And it drained me. It's gotten easier after sobriety. I have grown a lot as a person over the past five years, and maybe writing all this down and confronting my past played a role in that. Still, I keep having these morning thoughts that it's going to be the lost book that no one ever sees. I'd almost like to try to DIY it with a burlap cover and send all eight copies around the world. Or put my only copy in a plastic container and throw it in the Pacific Ocean. A year later it washes up in Japan or Korea and someone publishes it as a curiosity. What title would they give it? Maybe something like *Confessions of a Fool* or *The Big Man Laughed*. Somehow Morrissey gets a copy, plagiarizes a few words, and then a few people might begin clamoring for it.

It's the first thing I think about when I wake up in the morning. Occasionally, as I'm getting myself going, I'll listen to music on YouTube. There was a period where it seemed like before every song there was a commercial about opioid dependency. Torture. Especially for someone like me, with my background. It makes you want to scream—or take opioids!

One thing that concerns me is that my relationship with Mary feels like it's stagnating. Not that it's on its last legs, but it feels like it's on cruise control and running out of gas. We're very supportive of each other but it feels like we've drifted apart. We're still close but there isn't as much communication as there used to be. Maybe that's the natural course in long relationships? There's a spark missing now, but maybe it'll come back. At least there is stability in our daily routines and I can see some benefit in that.

My life is pretty hectic now, with so much crazy stuff going on, but this book is a priority, and I need to get it done in case I get hit by a car or something and it's not done. Fuuuck. That's how ghosts are made. Pissed-off ghosts. I'm worried that a meteor is gonna fall out of the sky and I won't see it coming. Cementing my soul to be walking the world of the unpublished for eternity.

Close calls. There have been many over the years. I swallowed gasoline as a tyke, but my grandmother's quick-thinking and fast action saved me. I was pursued by a creep in a van when I was a kid, but I didn't get in the van and wind up a corpse tossed in a ditch. I have OD'd multiple times, including the time the filmmaker gave me mouth-to-mouth and resuscitated me. Paramedics have saved me more than once. Then there was the bad case of tetanus and other maladies. I've survived hard living on the street, brutal fights against behemoths, death threats, van accidents. I've described some of these near-fatalities in detail, but there were many others. Hospitals have had me sign waivers in the event that I lose organs, digits, or even my life, basically saying you (or your loved ones) can't sue if we kill you. Are they imagining I will come back to haunt them as a ghost?

A guy asked me the other day if there was a close call that stands above all, one that I think about the most? Yes, there is. It happened when I was sixteen and caught a ride hitch-hiking.

I was dropped off at a highway off-ramp. Upon exiting the vehicle, I started walking backward while thanking the driver. I remember him saying, "Be careful," but as I was ambling away with my mind in another place, I walked backward into the freeway lane. I was totally sober, but I was lost in my own world. "Look out!" he screamed as I turned to face a car charging at seventy miles per hour. I started to run as fast as I could but only had a couple of seconds. The car swerved to avoid me and missed me by inches, spinning off the road past the shoulder into gravel. It's a miracle I wasn't clipped. If the driver hadn't reacted so quickly and skillfully, or if I had frozen, I would have been flattened. This scene has replayed over and over in my head hundreds of times.

For once, I'm not procrastinating. I gotta put this story down before my luck runs out. Have I used up my nine lives? Am I living on borrowed time? Once I joked to Tom, "I don't know what life will bring, but it will be fucked." Then we laughed. But I'm determined to work overtime to see this through. I would like to hurry and finish this book, but then again I would also like to win the lottery. Not to mention have the world experience everlasting peace. Hah! I just want to get it down before Armageddon. It's just that I'm overwhelmed with so much shit at the moment. One thing after another. When it rains, I'm waterboarded. If the pendulum is swinging, when she swings back, it's gonna be grape-peeling time. Bad. Horrible. I see the light. Please tell me that you see it too?

19

After a long hiatus, I decided to put together a new version of the band in 2018. We would do a few mini US tours and went to Europe a couple of times. We quickly became road warriors. I know the cycle of breaking up and getting back together can come across as comical, but at least we weren't doing it for drug money. We missed playing, recording, the road, each other. Music is the motor. It is not meant to be a long-term permanent reunion, but I'm expecting we'll play into late 2019. Let's see where it takes us. When that's done, I'll be ready for whatever's next. But first things first.

Life isn't always great but it looks like it is all we have. They say where there's life, there's hope. But some people are wound so tight right now. We always have a choice. Some people get out, some people go on. Some struggle, and some have their whole lives ahead of them. My friends and loved ones die, and I feel like I'll never figure it out. Then, there is some reflection and maybe a brief moment of clarity, and then on to the next distraction. Everything goes in circles. It's all been done before. Well, maybe not everything. The more things change…and life goes on. For now.

Wrecking. Burning. Sure, it's sexy and fun to destroy shit when you're a kid, but it's so much harder to create something. It's a challenge and that's what keeps me going forward right now. Like the man said, "Anybody can burn down these colleges and institutes of education, but how many would it take to build one?" Sometimes the old statues need to be torn down. If we don't do it, nature eventually will. I could die right now and I feel like I've done enough. I almost feel satisfied. I'll probably continue to play some kind of music, since that is what I've been doing all my life. Hearing music, feeling something, and flooding your emotions with that incredible sensation is one thing, but playing and making music and giving birth to that art, that is a feeling that is indescribable. I haven't done everything that I would like to do, but I have done more than I thought I would when I was sixteen years old.

My only real regret right now, today, is what we're leaving behind for the next generations. My sister and brother overcame the same or worse odds than I had. They were there too. I was old enough to run and get out, but they were stuck. I couldn't smuggle my little brother away from the abuse when he was eight years old, and it will always break my heart. How he and my sister both didn't wind up repeating this cycle, or getting loaded, jumping into a bottle, or jumping off of a bridge is a miracle in itself. But they both grew up healthy and had families of their own. I'm an uncle now. The abuse I suffered at the hands of my uncle stops here. I don't know the first thing about raising children—I can barely handle my dogs and my tribe who sit around our table—I just know that I love them and would protect them with my life. They're beautiful and fantastic little people. They have to keep going, long after we're gone, and afterward their kids will inherit this earth. So, we either change or we keep going downhill. Our schools should be places of mind expansion, not detention centers. Knowledge is power. Writing all this down, I came to realize that my parents weren't villains, they were just kids who were having kids of their own and had no idea what they were doing. What they did with that afterward is a different story. We all have to answer for our own shit.

But if anything can be taken from this story to relate to the future, it's that it's hopefully never too late. Change is the only constant. Yeah, yeah, I know. It's not roses. It never has been. I'm still a dick, but I tried to stop being an asshole a while ago—and there's a difference. I would hate to end this book thinking that it was written by an asshole. The story isn't over. I'm the same guy; I'm just trying different things. Some different things, some things are still habits. It will probably be that way for the rest of my life: to try, to fall, to get up, and try again. Tripping and falling. Fuck, I trip. I tripped on some mushrooms and DMT a short while ago. I'm an old goddamn man. Forty years old is the old age of youth, fifty years old is the youth of old age. I still drink, but I finally got off of the methadone program. These days, I see an addiction specialist. I still love seeing and hearing music. But I also know that everything should come in moderation these days. I had a seizure about a week ago also that scared the shit out of me, but this life has always been scary. The music, drugs, life, fun, sadness, death, struggle, confusion, love, and hate, it's all still there. I experience it every day. It never stops; that's why I get up in the morning. And maybe I'll write another book about it. And I'll say this one last time. Bullshit.

20

THAT LAST CHAPTER WAS ORIGINALLY going to be the end of the book. But then there was major upheaval in my life, and I'm not sure where it's heading. Things are chaotic, intense, up in the air, and I have no idea where I will land after it plays out. Maybe life's one long struggle in the dark, and it seems like I have both nothing to lose and everything on the line. I guess we'll soon see.

Though there was a half-hearted attempt a decade ago that went nowhere, I really started writing this book in earnest a little over four years ago, in the fall of 2015. There were false starts at the outset, but then I just dove in. It meant looking closely in the rear view mirror. But my world has changed drastically since then, and I'm still trying to process it all. If I were writing a novel, I'd know the ending I was working toward. It'd be all mapped out. This is different. I don't know where it's heading or how things will go.

When I look back over my life, it seems like it happened to another person. It's weird that I made it this far, considering. I don't blame anyone else for the hand I was dealt. Honestly, I do believe in fate, and that our paths are marked for us, and there's not much we can do about it. Fate. Destiny. I also think there's a balance in the universe and everybody has to sing the blues sometimes. Everybody can't be happy all the time, just like everybody isn't miserable all the time. Today it's me, tomorrow it'll be you. I feel like I've lived a full life. I could die a happy (or at least content) man right now, but I'm not ready to give it up yet. In my little corner of life, I feel like I've seen a lot, done a lot, shot a lot, laughed and cried a lot. But ya know what? This story is far from over. Just when you think you've done it all, the Skylab of all surprises drops on you like a house in the *Wizard of Oz*. Out of the blue, falling head over heels in love. Something the tough guys used to laugh about.

I've talked about girlfriends breaking your heart, walking in on them fucking one of your best friends. Stepping on your feelings just because someone once did it to them. Some people are sadistic and get enjoyment out of seeing people hurt. But you'll never know if it suits you if you never try and if you don't listen to what the heart wants. Never. Until it slaps you like you're running through an iron gauntlet. Sometimes, I feel completely relaxed and even ecstatic. Look both ways but you'll never see it coming. Then I feel like I can't breathe. A big, king-size sucker punch. A heap of them. And man, oh, man, is it a motherfucker. Along with Death, THEE big daddy. Sure, young, smartass me laughed about it, wrote half-hearted jokes about it, teased my friends when they were damn near suicidal over a woman. And now it's got me. Ain't karma a bitch?

But I'm not alone with this dilemma. Once bitten, you would have to be a reptile not to go crazy. It's beaten bigger and stronger men than me. Samson? The guy with the long hair and the weakness for beautiful Philistine women? Wars have been fought, the most honest poetry has just flowed out effortlessly, just by letting go and expressing how you feel. Words that sound like magic. It has brought people back to life and it has also crushed every ounce of joy and light out of others. I don't know where I am, literally. I don't know how I feel. I know it's got me. And if you think being strung out in a run-down squat is a tough hole to dig yourself out of, well, this is a different degree of difficulty. This is a much stronger challenge. A feeling that is so much purer and more overwhelming. Like an addiction, and like hate, it's something that doesn't sleep. Something that never gets tired. So you can't fight it, because you'll never win. Just pray and hope that it doesn't kill you. Hope that you're the chosen one that was spared. Saved by happiness and when cupid took aim and shot that arrow, it didn't hit an artery. And also, like dope, the feeling is complete bliss.

You'll do anything for it. Happy, excited, paranoid, sad, insane, it's definitely an E-ticket ride. At the moment, I'm feeling pretty good. But I have no idea what tomorrow will bring. Ya guard yourself and close it off from the world, but just open that door a crack, and like a beam of light that shines in, that light also casts a huge shadow. It will get you, it will save you, it loves you or it might kill you. So, do I sound ambivalent? Yeah, of course. People are born with a defense mechanism that protects you as you get older. After you have been burned once or twice, you don't keep sticking your hand in the fire. Is it better to have loved and lost than to become a cynical old man and drink yourself to death? Do you think I have the fucking answer? Honestly, I really don't like writing this when I feel so vulnerable. But this book has been an experiment in letting go and telling the truth. I haven't lied about anything in this book.

The people I name, the people I outed for behaving like animals or fucking in the mud amongst the pigs, they know I held my punches. They know there is much more INSANE, CRAZY SHIT I could bring up. And, honestly, if I get pushed into a corner by anyone questioning anything that they say is bullshit, bring it on. I spared you the first time. There's a lot worse to be told, if you want me to lay it all out.

My worst? Being a nasty person on the edge of being a bastard, a thug, a junkie, and a criminal. Now I'm feeling like I've found love and happiness. At least, that's how I feel at this moment. It does change every hour. Do I deserve to be happy? Fuck, your guess is as good as mine, but I'm following what I think is right. And you can't win if you don't play, right? It's in the stars, it's in the cards, spin the wheel, but nothing comes easy. Again, vulnerability, whenever I'm away from this person, I feel sick. But I'll do whatever I can to make this work. It's one of those things, no matter how hard I try to explain it here, unless you've been through this before, it's impossible to describe.

All right, how's this, I've been playing music since I was fifteen years old. Recently, the MC5 came to my town and I was asked by one of the members if I wanted to get up and sing a song with them. That might sound like a no-brainer. After all, I've dug this band since I first heard them as a teenager. But you have to remember what's going on in my heart right now. I had an opportunity to maybe spend a few minutes with the person who is the object of my infatuation. Maybe talk, maybe touch, maybe be with them. To me, that was the no-brainer. I passed on singing with the MC5 and stood in the shadows with my heart pounding like a drum. This cold, calloused heart that once beat like a snake's heart has started to warm up and pump vigorously. So I feel I deserve this, I deserve everything I get. Fuck it, I'm gonna fight for it, I'm gonna do whatever I have to do. If it kills me, I guess there are worse ways to die.

Wish me luck, because this story has just begun, this new part of my life has just begun, and I feel that I have just started to live. Maybe I'll tell ya how it turns out later.

AFTERWORD

SO, I SAID AT THE OUTSET that this was a suicide note to a suicide that never happened. Now, let me explain. I've always been sickened by how when someone dies, that in addition to people coming out of the woodwork to say how much they loved that person, the stories begin. The exaggerations. Even before the body is cold. At Tom's funeral a week after his passing, I started hearing the lies. But by then it's too late. What are you gonna do? Argue with the rumors and hearsay?

I've sang about suicide before because I've known people who killed themselves. I never thought that I would live forever, but I never thought I would be the one to pull the trigger, the one to be in charge and make the decision when I thought it was time. As I was writing this memoir, I thought it was my time to go. Again, nothing depressing, no sadness. I was actually happy, and calm, and felt a sense of relief. I was living with my ex-wife, who at one time was my go-to person. I thought we'd grow old together and die together. But after a while those bulbs burned out. I tried to talk with her about it, but she wasn't listening. She never had any interest in discussing problems. She either said I was being dramatic or would acknowledge my depression but said I should start taking medication to numb those feelings.

What was I feeling? I felt I'd gone as far as I could. I didn't see anything up ahead. I'd done everything I wanted to do.

There was nothing else. Numerous times, I had pulled out of tailspins and lived to tell about it. I know what it's like to get death threats because I've stood up to racist thugs. I've done enough drugs to OD multiple times. But I've also been around the world multiple times because of music. I've met thousands of people through my bands and made dozens of friends in countries that my music took me to. I started my own record label. I had a radio show. I wrote articles for magazines. I'd acted in a couple of indie movies made on shoestring budgets. I did a television commercial. I promoted and put on live concerts. I climbed mountains, fought and lost, loved and won, and did exactly whatever the fuck I wanted to do. I figured I had done everything. Since there was nothing left, I might as well quit while I was ahead.

I had always been fascinated by the siege of Masada. Instead of letting your enemy take your life, you steal their thunder and victory. You off yourself before they can snuff ya out. I love life, don't get me wrong, but I figured this world will get you one way or another and no one gets out alive. I didn't want to be in hospice or find myself washing dishes for the fifth time in one day and dropping dead.

Here's what I had envisioned. I wanted to tell my story, the goddamn truth, have a big festive party, and then do it. Just pull the plug. I rented a storage space in preparation and I slowly filled it with my prized possessions. I wasn't going to leave a mess that someone else would get stuck having to clean up. I'm very considerate in that regard. I would be organized in death. I started leaving envelopes around the storage space, addressed to different people. It would identify who got what. Mind you, I didn't have a lot to leave, but I wanted my friends to have certain guitars and other things to remember me by. I wanted all my possessions to go where they'd be appreciated. I took a friend to my storage space and told him if anything were to happen to me, this is where all my treasures were. As soon as this book was finished and published and my side of the story was told, I was gonna make sure to get him the spare key.

But I stress this fact, I wasn't the slightest bit sad or upset. I felt free. My "relationship" had become nothing. All was not blissful at home. The person I was with wasn't really living. She was constantly planning way ahead, not living in the moment, and obsessing about death. She even bought us matching burial plots, right next to each other for eternity. There was a point where I thought the book would be finished and then I could carry out my goodbye party. But, like they say, if you want to hear God laugh, announce your plans. Hey, maybe I've already used that line a couple of times, but there's a reason.

So the unexpected did happen. I was walking my dogs one afternoon (one of the few things that still gave me any joy) and as we were passing through a school playground, I came across a bag of garbage. Not normal garbage. Portland garbage. Shitty underwear, syringes, rotten food, and a couple of dildos. When my dogs made a beeline for it and started rummaging through it, I flipped the fuck out. I immediately called a friend who was always on some kind of neighborhood watch page on social media and asked her what to do. She gave me the name and number of a woman who dealt with that kind of mess every day. She was fighting with the city's homeless advocates, who treated the people who threw around shit and syringes like children. She helped elderly people whose front yards had been taken over by homeless camps. She would moderate town hall meetings with the people who had sold this city to the developers and call them out in public forums. She was a spark plug. She gave me a number to call and the trash was gone the next day. I thanked her and we started communicating regularly.

And then, one day, we met in person. And the bulbs turned back on. I never saw this coming. But love is like that. You don't call the shots, and you have no control over it.

But there was a wrinkle. She was married to an abusive bully who didn't give two shits about what she did. It was kind of like my situation, when I'd ask my once significant other to talk about not feeling the love anymore only to be told to take a pill. Her husband flat-out refused to talk about it. That is, until she said she was moving out. This was the beginning of a whole new story. It's the same story that has been told many times over centuries. A never-ending crazy story. There were obstacles you would not believe. Drama turned up to ten. Screaming and crying from both sides. Midnight rendezvous. Threats of violence. If a girlfriend's jealous ex wants to threaten to chop my balls off, well, I've heard worse. There was passion, love, trust, and romance like I had never experienced in my life. Anything that is truly great and worth its salt never comes easy. That would be a huge understatement. I never saw this coming. I was planning my going-away party one month, and six months later, I was planning my wedding.

And, yes, I would get married. On Valentine's Day, no less. At City Hall. The wedding itself was very simple. The reception we later held to celebrate it was a grand event, elaborately planned down to the last detail. Well over a hundred people attended and we pulled out all the stops. It took a lot of effort, but it was worth it, and our many guests seemed to have a blast. This has been an amazing year, with many plans for the next one. We'd like to buy a house with a yard where I could plant lots of rose bushes. I'd like to give away bouquets of roses to our friends. We want to renew our vows, maybe at a place called The Grotto, which is a pretty unique setting in Portland. There's a lot we want to do, including traveling down to Mexico. Will I really go parasailing in the Yucatán Peninsula?

It feels like I have crammed five to ten years of living inside twelve months. One major change is that I try to enjoy the little things. Stop and smell the roses may sound like a cliché, but there's a reason people flock to watch the cherry blossoms every spring. In my case, I went to an amazing field of tulips with my wife and now we want to go back every year. I guess humans can't stop all the flowers from blooming, as much as we may try.

The band would get back together and play around the world. There were many highlights from another European tour, and that included getting time to travel with my new bride inside places like Spain and Ireland. A working honeymoon. Touring exposes you to new things you wouldn't otherwise see. And I got to share that with her. One thing that happened a few times in Europe was having old friends become overcome with emotion upon seeing me. It was very unexpected. I think of a dear friend in London who seemed especially touched that I was doing well. He probably figured my health would deteriorate like Tom's had and that I would grow bitter and grumpy. Instead, I was happy, healthy, and quick to laugh. My only regret was not having the book finished and out. I could have sold a thousand, easy. People were asking about it non-stop.

Traveling through Europe, I often became engaged in conversation with strangers, people from all backgrounds and walks of life who seemed to have their shit together. To get an outside perspective, I would ask them what they thought of America. Usually it would go something like, "We're kind of embarrassed for you. Your current government is so fucked-up that you are becoming clowns. You're hurting Europe and the rest of the world with your misguided policies. What happened to your best and brightest? The US has given the world so much cool art and culture that it's a shame you are becoming known for your stupidity. How did you allow this to happen?" These people really respected us for our entertainers, subcultures like the hippie movement, scientific breakthroughs, modern technological advances, entrepreneurial spirit, numerous inventions and innovations, constitutional freedoms, and being a nation of immigrants. Just in terms of music, America has given the world so much: jazz, blues, country, bluegrass, folk, rock, hip-hop, and Broadway. But now they see us as a nation of confused leaders and shameful policies. They question our motives. I hear what they're saying. I tell them that tens of millions of disappointed and frustrated Americans feel the same way, and that if it gets much worse I might not want to be buried on American soil.

There were so many unexpected things in the past year. For example, I mentioned earlier some bands that had covered our songs. Well, you can add Metallica to the list. They covered "Taken by Surprise" at the big arena in downtown Portland. That song I had written in ten minutes in a Chicago hotel room. I never could have imagined it when I was scalping backstage passes to their concert for drug money twenty-five years earlier. It would have been a real long shot. Something even more unexpected and meaningful came about when kids in a local School of Rock program decided to cover Portland bands. They were learning cool songs like "Over the Edge" by the Wipers, and PI was one of the bands selected. It really caught me off guard. The song they chose was "Just to Get Away." I watched the kids rehearse and later I watched them perform in concert, and they did a really good job. I just had one question for them. There is some profanity in that song, and I asked if that was a problem. Their answer? "Oh, no, we *like* it!"

There would be more medical issues and a slew of procedures. A bronchitis-like chest infection that produced crackling sounds, a virulent super-mutant strain of cold or flu, hernia surgery, throat surgery, a dental bridge, and one more painful than all of those combined. How can I describe it? I remember being bed-ridden and shaking like a leaf. Shee-it, I was afraid to try to shit! Alive, getting stronger, but definitely using lockjaw as a comparison for pain. As soon as the heavy-duty meds wore off, the pain was excruciating. It was beyond being tender to the touch. When I went under the knife, I thought I'd be back at work the next day, running around, making my rounds and doing my business. Nope. Even though I have a high pain threshold, this had me docked. It felt like my eyes were spinning in my sockets. I don't think it's age. I think it's just someone going into your nut with a scalpel and rooting around and ripping stuff out. A new scar that the coroner will one day see. I can only wonder what the motorcycle daredevil Evel Knievel, another one-time Montana boy, looked like on the slab. I think I'm catching up.

And one thing I didn't even mention was how stressful it was to even get that surgery done. I had jumped through all the hoops only for the insurance company to call the day before the surgery was scheduled and deny coverage. It meant having to cancel the surgery at the last minute and start the whole process over again. It meant having to play shows in pain without resorting to self-medicating. I got on the phone, my new wife got on the phone, there were more visits to the doctors' office, it took time, but I finally got it straightened out. It's like that with me. It always feels like I choose the wrong checkout lane.

So I'm alive, ready to move forward. I'm shutting down the band at the end of this year. It's been a good run. There's a lot I want to do. It could be short-term or long-term, part-time or full-time, but one thing I'm planning on doing is helping people in need. I have something lined up with a non-profit where I'll be working on behalf of the disadvantaged, including folks who are homeless, developmentally challenged, elderly, or struggling in some way. I'm sure I want to do something creative as well, maybe writing more or doing a solo music project. Local bands have invited me to go in the studio and put down vocals, so I expect there will be collaborations in the near future.

I sometimes think back to my band's humble beginnings. We were all kids from broken families. We came from nothing. My bandmates became family to me, we became a band of brothers. There was loyalty and brotherhood. As I said in the documentary, when I realized this, it was like a puzzle was solved. Over the years, I've had roughly thirty bandmates in Poison Idea. If we got everyone together it would be a massive family reunion.

Our final shows are set. And I'm excited about them. One major thing is that we have booked a tour of Japan. We've been hoping to get back for fifteen years. The initial plan was that we would play one final show after we got back, and had settled on LA. At that time, a friend of mine from Staten Island was trying to get us to come play in NYC, but when I told him we had decided on LA instead, he said, "Fuck LA, New York deserves better." It was a good line. Then, when the LA show fell through, we started aiming for NYC—just as long as it could be set up to take place by the end of the calendar year. That was the main determining factor.

When I reformed the band, I had told the guys that we'd play as many interesting shows as we could in 2019, but that would be it. I suspect some of them will be melancholy when we walk off the stage for the last time. I can understand why, because there is still something left in the tank. We're playing well. But I'd rather end it a month too soon than a year too late.

I'm wearing more hats now: I'm not just the singer and front person. I'm the tour manager, the road manager, the stage manager, I arrange the flights and book the hotels, and I man the merch table. I won't say it takes a toll, but it's not like all I have to do is sing and do the occasional interview.

As I'm writing this, we are about to take off for Japan for a whirlwind week of gigs. For fifteen years I've wanted to go back to experience more of the country and give a better account of myself than I did the first time. When the offer finally came, we took it. Then we play Seattle next month, right before Xmas. It will be our last Northwest show, and I imagine some people will make the drive up from Portland or down from BC for the gig. Our final shows ever will be the last weekend of the decade. Those two shows will take place in Brooklyn. That's fitting. Because it was a NYC band from one of the outer boroughs—namely the Ramones from Forest Hills, Queens—who sold me on punk rock in the first place.

One thing I meant to mention earlier is that when I perform I feel free to make changes to my lyrics. It's a way of keeping the songs fresh. I'm still doing that, and likely will on these final gigs. Sometimes, changes may be so subtle that no one would notice. Or it could be a very dramatic change that would be obvious to anyone familiar with the song. I like playing around with my lyrics, updating them, making them current, or making them more poetic. I've always liked to improvise and try new things. It keeps the songs from getting stale. It's almost like I want to reanimate these old songs and bring them to life. Or it's like trying to perfect an early draft.

Someone once asked me to write down the words to one of my early songs, "Lifestyles." I sat down and wrote it out in my best penmanship, as I was hearing the music in my head. Later, when the person listened to the song with this handmade lyric sheet, he noted lots of small changes, which he thought only improved the recorded version. I've always thought it was strange that a songwriter could knock out a song in fifteen minutes and then sing it the exact same way for decades. Especially if they just slapped together a few words or strung together a few nonsensical phrases to meet a recording deadline. My mentality: it's not set in stone. You can play around and have fun. Why not make improvements if you can? I've always thought songs can evolve. You can change it to improve it.

This book started off with ancient history, back when my parents got together, and it's moved from the distant past up toward the present. All along, I held up a mirror to myself. Have I always liked what I saw? No way. But I do feel like I have grown during the writing of this book and come to terms with painful memories of my past. Without a doubt. There are many things I would not have thought about and learned from if I had not gone through this exercise.

I try to see all the angles, but I can't always. Sometimes, you just gotta go with your gut. When you let too much doubt creep in, you're opening the door for failure. Be yourself, even if your presence may come across as different or outsized to others. A lion doesn't have to announce that it is a lion. It just is. *Enjoy* your life.

It helps to put things in historical perspective. Bigger things have probably happened. Every generation has its struggles. My grandparent's generation was up against the Spanish Flu, the Great Depression, the Dust Bowl, WWII, and had patients with extreme cases of polio living in "iron lungs." They had it rough, but they are known as the "Greatest Generation." It's easy to imagine a time in the near future when the sirens are non-stop, and we'll all have to buckle down. The biggest event in my lifetime is 9/11. Maybe something else will come along soon to eclipse that. Future generations will have their own catastrophes which surpass it. Natural disasters, epidemics, genocides, wars that bomb cities into dust. But then think of the Black Death, the plague that wiped out half of Europe's population in the 1300s. What can compare to that? Try to keep things in perspective. It's easy to get down thinking about the state of things. But if you hang around doomsayers, you're gonna cry black.

CODA

Last Words (I Swear)

THE BOOK WAS TO END with Tom's death, but I have sketched out a few broad brushstrokes of what would follow. I may never get around to writing it all down, but trust me when I say that it has been a wild and crazy ride, without any signs of slowing down.

I still find myself thinking of Tom every day. More than music or movies, what I most would have wanted to talk with him about are things I come across that I find funny. It could be a standup routine by Greg Giraldo, a comedy sketch from Dave Chappelle, an interview on *The Howard Stern Show*. When I heard Doug Stanhope for the first time, I thought maybe he's not punk, but he's shared some of the same life experiences. He's a "trasher" and would fit right in with my musician friends. He had a similar attitude as us, and I'm pretty sure Tom would have considered him a kindred soul. When I discover something new or interesting in the arts, one of my first thoughts is "would Tom have dug it?" Then I feel bad that he is missing out on cool new stuff I'd have wanted him to check out. I also miss describing crazy things from my day-to-day life. I'd want to run that stuff by him and see what he thought. That's when I miss him most.

In *Legacy of Dysfunction*, Tom tried to sum up what mattered to him: "Being in the band gave my life meaning. You live your life and you die. I'll leave behind a tombstone or a bag of ashes and a few recordings that people can look at that I contributed to. As an artist, you leave something behind. What you leave behind is what you created, and I helped create Poison Idea." That he did. And in the process he was a great friend to me.

It's now late December, and we're back from Japan. The shows were really good and we were treated great. First-class. We played with good bands, including the legendary Systematic Death. It was awesome not being strung-out this time, performing sober and feeling more in control. The band was locked in and played with laser focus. It was what I had wanted. I saw a lot more of the country than the first time and I noticed many new things. I could probably write a long travelogue. But not here. My wife was with me, and it was like continuing the honeymoon. Another continent on our around-the-world tour. She and I just put together our first Xmas cards. It consisted of twelve snapshots from 2019; it starts with a picture of us holding our marriage certificate and ends with me next to her, dressed as Santa.

The period between returning from Tokyo and playing in Seattle five or six weeks later was intense and could fill many pages. But I'll skip ahead and cut to the chase. The Seattle show went well, and it felt like the perfect tune-up for our upcoming NYC shows—which brings me to this weekend. We arrived at JFK yesterday afternoon and hit the ground running. The missus and I immediately began covering a lot of turf, seeing the sites and visiting cool shops. It's right after Christmas and the city is decked out with holiday themes: the big Xmas tree at Rockefeller Center and the famous window displays at the major department stores. We saw all that somewhere between eating at the famous oyster bar at Grand Central Station and going downtown to Battery Park. It's a few days before the New Year's Eve madness at Times Square, when the ball will drop to mark the end of one decade and the start of another. The city is packed with tourists ready to bring it in with a loud roar. There's a buzz in the air.

It's Saturday afternoon and after a full day of soaking up as much of the city as possible with limited hours, we just got to the club in Brooklyn. It's the first of two shows this weekend. Tonight Bushwick, tomorrow Greenpoint. The venues are on the small side, but both are sold out. The band is excited about being here. Really stoked. I think we're primed to have two good shows. Some people are coming in from hundreds of miles away. My friend Alex just got in from Boston. It'll be nice to hang out with him, along with other friends coming from places like Ithaca and Pittsburgh. There are also a lot of people who were at our first area shows in 1990, and it will be nice to see them. Pillars of the scene. I'll get to catch up with a lot of people. Well, it's time for me to start putting some thought into tonight's set list. I'll probably wing it, but we'll do a Roky Erickson song and maybe the Gism cover the band learned for Japan. It'll be a long night. I'll write more tomorrow. I do want to finish the book before the band sets foot onstage tomorrow night.

It's early Sunday evening. Last night's show was fun. People came out of the woodwork. The sound wasn't perfect, but overall it sure felt good, and I would have liked to have kept playing much longer. The vibe in the room was great. One down, one to go.

From a logistical standpoint, tonight's show should be pretty easy. The promoter has been generous and arranged a very nice hotel room for my wife and I just a block or two from the venue. We just went out with friends for good Italian food in Williamsburg, and then headed back to the hotel to change and get ready. Earlier in the day, we went to MoMA. We saw famous works by Picasso, Van Gogh, and others. I'm not sure if any of their great art will inspire me tonight, but here's hoping. Actually, I've already got all the inspiration I'll ever need.

During dinner conversation, it dawned on me that the band might have played more shows in NYC than in any city outside Portland. My dinner companions could list eight in the city. If you factor in Long Island, and count my stint on air at WFMU across the river in NJ, it rises to double digits. So, in a way, this city is kind of our home away from home. That's a cool thought. Our second home. I hope we'll deliver tonight. We want to go out on a high note. I've been thinking about the set list over the course of the day. We have a large catalog and I want to play a lot of different songs tonight. Maybe we'll play four to five of the standard crowd-pleasers that we played last night, but the rest will be different. Some diehards got tix for both nights and maybe they'll be able to appreciate the variety. "New York deserves better." Indeed. It's almost thirty-nine years to the day after the first Poison Idea show and now it's almost time for the last. One song we will do from last night is the Roky cover: "You're Gonna Miss Me." Will I get choked up? Maybe, but I suspect I'll be too busy having a blast. I won't tell you how tonight's show goes. I'll save that for another time. Or a book I may never write.

The music stuff is always going to be there, but the life that surrounds it is much more interesting. People who know me understand that the stories behind the music are the fuel and that music comes second. And considering that I planned to write this book, see it published, and then hang myself? I think redemption, confession, and atonement are definitely themes. And now that I've written the last chapter and my life has spun 180 degrees, that's how I see it. A long suicide note that had a surprise happy ending.

Saved by the bell at the last second. And I have nothing against letting people know this book was once intended to be my farewell. Truth is always best.

What would I have done differently? Many people prepare for old age, while other people can't be bothered. They don't need any security. Me? I would have taken more chances. I would have tried to make myself happy by following my heart and letting go.

I want to live like people used to, when they would throw caution to the wind and fly to Mexico for both a weekend divorce and a new marriage. Hotter than a pepper sprout. I'd rather live one more day that happened to be the best day of my life than to live a thousand more empty days. "I want to live." That is where I am now. Ready for the next step.

Brooklyn 12/29/2019